# COVID-19 AND | KILLING CONSPIRACY THEORIES

Also written by Simon Chilembo:

When the Mighty Fall – *Rise Again Mindgames*

Machona – *Emigrant*

Machona Awakening – *Home in Grey Matter*

Machona Son – *Ain't Going Nowhere*

Machona Blogs – *As I See It*

Machona Mother – *Shebeen Queen*

# COVID-19 AND I | KILLING CONSPIRACY THEORIES

## SIMON CHILEMBO

Published by
CHILEMBO Media Storytelling Books
Huitfeldts gate 17
0253 Oslo, Norway
simon@chilembo.com
www.chilembo.com

**Covid-19 and I: Killing Conspiracy Theories**

ISBN Print: 978-82-692152-0-5



Typeset by Andrea Willmore
Cover design by Andrea Willmore
Cover photograph by Simon Chilembo
Book production by YesPress

**Saul Sulayman Sowe**


If we are brothers

Our belly buttons

Shall tingle in each other's presence

If I see reflections of my mother

In the aura of your mother around you

Then the deal is done

You are my brother

I love you by default


From poem *To Love a Man*,
by Simon Chilembo

Knowledge is power. Information is liberating. Education is
the premise of progress, in every society, in every family.

KOFI ANNAN

# CONTENTS

# INTRODUCTION

Sometime in February 2020, I sat and discussed concept development for my then new *Diaspora Magic Talks Show* programme on Inthemixstyle Radio with my former bosses, Karina Svendsen and Ariel Leficura. We soon came to dwell upon the then already globally rapidly spreading Coronavirus disease (COVID-19). At that time, the potentially devastating nature of the disease on a global scale was already apparent.

Given my thoughts around the disease and its likely overall impact on world society given the lockdown that had already taken place in China, the massive death tolls in Italy, and the erratic responses emerging from the USA, they encouraged me to do some work on the subject.

Ariel went further and challenged me to write a book with the theme of *how the realities and myths around Coronavirus disease (COVID-19) have impacted me.*

The book title "COVID-19 and I" arose from the challenge above. The title describes more an observational than experiential discourse because I have not contracted the disease thus far.

"Killing Conspiracy Theories" as a subtitle alludes to two perspectives:

- ADJECTIVE "killing" – Deaths attributable to misleading information spread by those that claim that COVID-19 is not real, and that the *myth* of the existence of the disease was created by certain forces that conspire to take over the world and curtail civil liberties. Hence *Conspiracy Theories.*

- TRANSITIVE VERB "killing" – My goal is, through scientific thought reasoning, to neutralize these Conspiracy Theories to a point of metaphoric death.

  I opt to share my thoughts and seek enlightenment with the open-minded layperson, or curious professional and intellectual appreciating fresh and original thinking. I leave confrontations with Conspiracy Theories peddlers to others; I can't stand the noise. I will, of course, respond accordingly to arising critiques and challenges.

The blog article **Should I Die**: *Covid-19 Reflections* (Chapter 16, pp. 72–80) came out during a private brainstorming process as to how I'd approach the writing of the new book. Parallel to thinking about, and subsequently embarking on the project, the following poems came forth:

- **The Unthinkable – 1** (Chapter 17, pp. 82–87)

- **Ripe Old Age – 1** (Chapter 18, pp. 88–91)

- **Sea of Possibilities – 1** (Chapter 19, pp. 92–96)

- **Fear No Darkness** (Chapter 20, pp. 97–98)

- **Freedom:** *To Die or Not to Die For* (Chapter 21, pp. 99–104)

- **Falsified:** *I Keep on Penning* (Chapter 22, pp. 105–106)

- **The Threshold** (Chapter 23, pp. 107–114)

Meanwhile, each day since the outbreak of the pandemic towards the end of 2019, I continued to receive numerous queries about my wellbeing on my social media platforms. All in my worldwide relations network assured me that they were coping well under the circumstances. That was good to hear. An enormous emotional relief.

Much concern arose regarding those that were confused and afraid. They were feeling helpless in a situation where nobody in the world had any universally acknowledgeable counter-strategy against the pandemic spread.

As the lockdowns in individual countries of the world began to earnestly roll out from March and onwards, full panic struck. The latter was indicated by both private messages and public postings on my personal social media platform spaces. Even total strangers featured here.

Postings contents included all kinds of information, advice, and warnings. These were often forwarded from just as all kinds of sources: dubious and genuine; non-traceable and traceable. There was, and there continues to be a preponderance of ludicrously outright outlandish, misleading, and potentially health and societal management dangerous information doing the rounds, though.

This book aims to help alleviate the fears so many people are feeling right now by sharing my thoughts, which I continue to clarify and formalise on my journey in pursuit of knowledge.

With this book, I hope to inspire reflection and critical thinking against all the fracas that we are currently constantly being bombarded with around Coronavirus disease (COVID-19). I highlight experiences of my life's journey and processes as the foundation for my discourse entry points, explanatory models, and philosophical postulates in given contexts.

I'm neither a medical doctor nor am I qualified in any allopathic medicine sciences. I do not wield any political or social control power either. Therefore, I am certainly not in a position to offer or suggest any cures for, or solutions as to how to manage the pandemic.

I am a thinker, I am a writer, I am a poet. Through my works, I address myself to the individual. Particularly with my poetry, I seek to stir emotions, inspire thought, and encourage action towards life-supporting choices.

Growing up as a child in Lesotho in the 1960s, I was ever amid traditional Basotho poetry recitals and songs called *mangae*. These are performances of ritual rites of passage into adulthood for boys and girls[1]. *Mangae* are a celebration of life in its totality. They have made a lasting impression on me, profoundly influencing my storytelling style and proclivity towards expressing my deepest thoughts and feelings through poetry.

The joys, trials, and tribulations of my life have long taught me to fear not the unknown. Higher formal education has taught me how to seek information, decipher and analyse it, discard the irrelevant, pick out and apply the relevant and true as to my goals.

Although the current Coronavirus disease (COVID-19) debacle has presented more challenging economic and social conditions worldwide, my personal experiences with the Global Financial Crisis of 2008 have toughened my skin some more. Therefore, I believe that I am competent enough to make a substantive theoretical and factual contribution to the debate on the theme covered in this book.

I have deliberately chosen not to state directly, if not confrontationally, any people names that feature prominently in the global Conspiracy Theories rigmarole, neither the proponents nor their objects of scorn. Both parties already occupy more than adequate space in the infinitely diverse world multi-media platforms as it is. However, a list of relevant references is given at the end of the book: Appendix, p. 129.

It is worth noting that all the references applied in this book are online-based.

Furthermore, it is not my intention to want to deliberately offend anybody, directly or indirectly. I have neither need nor reason to want to exalt anybody either. Nor is it my intention or

---

[1]  Art & Life in Africa, *Visual Symbols of Self: South Sotho Arts and Initiation*, Riep, DMM, Author, https://bit.ly/3gucIT5, (accessed 23 August 2020)

wish to directly or indirectly expose anyone to personal danger, or disadvantage in their professional standings or prospects thereof.

## BOOK STRUCTURE

The unusual structure of the book – combination of direct address, blogs, poetry, and verbatim video scripts – is a reflection of the extent to which the subject has stimulated my creative potential. It was a spontaneous process about which I could not do much but adhere to. I hope the reader shall find the book format enjoyable.

Below is an edited transcript of my first of three off-the-cuff public responses to the Coronavirus disease (COVID-19) pandemic ramifications. I just had to speak there and then:

### EDITED TEXT OF IMPROMPTU INTRODUCTION TALK TO SHOULD I DIE: COVID-19 REFLECTIONS YOUTUBE VIDEO: 18/03-2020[2]

In these hard Coronavirus times, I extend my heart to everyone in the world. I hope and wish that everyone is living well and strong. Those who are ill, those who've got health issues that are compounded by the virus, I wish you a speedy recovery.

Coronavirus has caused a crisis in the world economy reminiscent of the 2008 Global Financial Crisis from which I got a knock that I have yet to recover from. So, those of you out there, I included, having a hard time losing jobs, or fearing job losses – because they are coming – losses of business as clients and everybody falls off, I feel for you.

Big, powerful incidents like this change everybody. We will be fine though. It's only a matter of time. We just have to be resilient

---

[2]  Simon Chilembo, SHOULD I DIE: COVID-19 REFLECTIONS, https:// youtu.be/YfJVi40uEZk (accessed July 03, 2020)

enough. When it's over, there's no guarantee that things will be the same as before. So, if suddenly you as an entrepreneur find that you are out of business, don't worry; that's a normal outcome.

The challenge is that many of us live from hand to mouth; it takes a long time to establish a solid private economic buffer. This is especially so in the Diaspora, where many of us first generations are on our own. We don't have any back-ups from some rich uncle. We depend on ourselves: our energy, our minds.

Therefore, when big things like this happen – stuff that we have no control over – when we get a knock, we get a knock.

From my personal experience, I can only advice, I can only suggest that everybody calm down. It is easier said than done. But I've been there. I've done it. After losing my business, my finances, and other material assets over five years (2008-2013), I survived the debilitating consequences of the 2008 Global Financial Crisis.

For example, all over the world, thousands of people suffered acute mental illnesses that culminated in a rise in suicides in many countries[3]. Embrace this situation because there's nothing you can do about it. All you can do, the stuff that you can control, is that you can breathe.

For as long as you live you can breathe. For as long as you can breathe you can control your feelings, you can control your thoughts.

"Think positive!" everybody says. Again, easier said than done. But you've got to be prepared that when things finally become alright again, you might rebuild your business. But it's not going to be the same. There's no guarantee that you'll have the same clients coming back to you. There's no guarantee that they'll be expecting the same kind of service. People come out with possibly transformed mindsets.

Remember that this thing hits everybody. Albeit with variable intensities according to the nature of business and its magnitude.

---

[3] Policy Bristol, *The 2008 Global Financial Crisis: effects on mental health and suicide,* Gunnell, D; Donavan, J; Barnes, M.; et al, Authors, https://bit.ly/3hFW43W (accessed 23 August 2020)

Some will reorganize and make strong comebacks eventually. Others will make slow, ever so vulnerable comebacks due to various factors, such as failure to reposition effectively in the new environment. Some might not even come back at all.

If you are in the last category and find that you just have no chance of rebuilding your business, you might have to find something else. You have to look for a job. In this new environment, the whole society – job market, business, organization management – changes continually. You cannot do much about that. The only thing that you can do is to control your-thoughts-and-your-feelings.

You might need expert help in psychology and personal change management, or counselling here. With an astute mind and good help from your family and network, it will be alright.

If it doesn't work out, i.e. you fail to rise, at least fall, or if you die, die fighting!

It doesn't matter what you think of yourself by way of being an influencer. You've got to remember that if you are somebody, somebody else somewhere is looking at you. They might not say it, they might not show themselves up. But somebody somewhere is looking at you for inspiration, for hope.

Hope keeps our dreams into perspective. Then, to fire up and actualize our dreams, we have faith. We say: 'Everything is gonna be alright!'

Faith is fuelled by things that we do to stay alive – the things that give us strength; tune-up our minds and keep our emotions alive.

When you need spiritual sustenance, you go to church: you read your Bible. Where applicable, you read your Koran; you read your Torah; you read the Bhagavad Gita. It doesn't matter what your belief is that feeds your faith.

You might derive strength from your family, your friends, your habits, your hobbies. The same might be achieved through reading, writing, or training – anything.

Do all those things. Never give up. Don't give up because this is a cycle. It just turns on and on and on: we'll fall, we'll rise; we'll fall, we'll rise. Sometimes we'll just keep rising and rising – it happens to some people. Good for them.

Some will fall and never rise again. That's tough. But whatever the case, whether we fall and stay there, or rise, there's always something to learn to help us move forward, or sustain the condition that we find ourselves in.

The most important thing is to embrace the idea that you can only be who and what you are. That's my philosophy. You can only do what you do. It's just the way it is.

You can have all these dreams of doing and achieving great things. But your launching pad is the condition where you are here and now: the things that you can do, the place where you are – that's the most important thing.

Know who you are. Know yourself. Know your capabilities here and now. And, based on that, you can project your potential; and that potential firing up, in return, your hopes – from hope to faith, and then from faith to the realization of your dreams.

For me, writing, which has culminated in my publishing six books since the second half of 2015, has helped me to tackle perhaps the most challenging time in my adult life.

**OTHER TALKS:**
- COVID-19: WE SHALL PULL THROUGH, Chapter 24, p. 116–119.
- COVID-19 PERSONAL COPING STRATEGIES, Chapter 25, p. 120–123.

August 23, 2020
Blog: www.chilembo.com
Twitter: @simonchilembo

# BOOK 1

# CONSPIRACY THEORIES
## My Take

# CHAPTER 1

❖

# BEEN THERE, DONE THAT
Global Financial Crisis 2008
Survival Attitude: Immortality

I had begun to bleed seriously by the northern summer of 2008. Northern autumn 2008 ushered in the Global Financial Crisis. The latter delivered the final blow. I fell flat on my stomach. Face smashed flat. My yet to heal abdominal hernia operation scar failed to split open. Thank goodness.

The operation scar was obtained from a procedure carried out in the spring of the previous year. Suffice to say that the pain was horrendous. Subsequently, I lost everything I owned of money and objects of affection and practical use.

My hard-earned wealth got erased almost overnight. The official declaration of personal bankruptcy five years later was the final slap on my already flattened face. Having physically healed by then, my belly held. But I felt finished. I could as well have died.

Alas, I recalled that my life is bigger than material trappings of man-made constructs of living on earth. Death could wait, therefore. In time I'd be fine and strong again, work and get my money back. I'd pay my debts and then live happily ever after in the continuous story that my soul writes on the numerous paths of the journeys of my life.

My life has journeyed over many planes of existence over many epochs. I have lived and died and lived and died and lived and died. I am not cognizant of where and when my life began. All I know is that I in this life opened my eyes to find a pendulum oscillating in long, breathe-taking swings.

I followed the swings over and over again until it dawned upon me that that was the flow and nature of my life: I'll rise, I'll fall, I rise, I'll fall, I'll rise on and on until I decide that I've had enough. I decided that if the pendulum was my life rhythm, I could as well own and control it.

The pendulum last swung to the extreme right, parallel to the ground. I made it pause there indefinitely whilst I allowed myself to die a little. I remain a dead man walking for as long as the pendulum stays where it is.

For I'm a living dead, I'm oblivious to pain. I'm oblivious to suffering. The day I stop moving, the pendulum shall succumb to gravity, fall, and continue with its eternal oscillations. I shall not help but awaken back to life with the pendulum because for it to live I have to breathe.

In essence, I am forever: I keep moving, I keep walking dead or alive. It's no big deal when I'm alive in the eyes of the world because life sees life by default. Forces that seek to kill me shall never vanquish the vital pendulum that perpetually oscillates my life alternately from light to no light, to light to no light to light every heartbeat pacing my respiratory rhythm.

My disappearance from the eyes of the wicked is an illusion of my death. It is ever so temporary. They may have struck and hit the soft spots that made me fall and seemingly die. They do not know, but for as long as the pendulum stands and swings, it'll only be a matter of time before I emerge again. Some say it's resurrection.

I cannot die for as long as the essence of my being, the pendulum, remains unscathed. But to harm the pendulum is to harm the self. Therefore, in good or bad times, I shall survive.

Always. That is the source of my fearlessness, my resilience. A dead man walking is indifferent to ecstasy or melancholy, attention, or lack of love or hate.

The only thing that matters to me is my freedom: the freedom to live as I choose to live. If I die, I'll die only because I make it possible. I hold my fate in my hands only for the world to see. The pendulum that is the essence of my life lies in spaces far remoter than any soul can ever fathom. Hack my hands off, I won't die.

# CHAPTER 2

# CORONAVIRUS DISEASE (COVID-19)
## Living with Economic Collapse Realities

Northern spring Coronavirus disease (COVID-19) is here. It is invisible. It is mysterious. Its ramifications are visible by the thousands of people it continues to kill the world over. Not to mention the near-collapse of the entire world economy. A new, more ruthless Global Financial Crisis 2020 is here. Northern autumn 2008 Global Financial Crisis is like little boys' money games play compared to this.

My lost flattened face still breathes, but the assumed healed abdominal hernia operation scar is active again, in all its 18-centimeter length from below my sternum to just before my navel ridge. Beneath the thick scar tissue, it feels like there is brought to life a thin electrical cord. The cord softly buzzes along with non-stop energy as if a guitar string that has forgotten to stop vibrating after the song is over.

Cramp-like sporadic twitches make their call every so often during the day. I liken these to electrical impulses seeking to converge and rebound at the midpoint of the operation scar. They are so powerful they cause me to yelp and bend over as if I've just been kicked in the stomach. This is very painful when I respond like a soul that knows no death. It is more painful than during the initial months of the 2008 Global Financial Crisis.

New pain on old pains can be a vicious experience.

Lastingly harmful as the first global financial crisis has been on me, I have yet to die as in the death of ordinary mortals who have never looked death in the eye before. It is the toughness of spirit that I have derived from the previous crisis that will carry me through this current one. The challenge is more daunting this time around, though: my life in its barest material possessions minimum is all I have on the frontline.

Having already battled financial ruin, I now lack the financial resources and monetary buffer that I need to help me withstand the effects of the Covid-19 pandemic. All I have to do is to make one small mistake and COVID-19 and its ramifications will be on my case. The virus attacks and kills even the mightiest of us all[4]. The economically weak, the poor, are as vulnerable as can be. As always. If that is the case, then who am I against the pandemic?

---

[4] Reuters, *Factbox: Prominent deaths linked to COVID-19*, Heavens, A, Author, https://reut.rs/3li2TLt, (accessed 26 August 2020)

# CHAPTER 3

## MY HERITAGE
### Source of Strength

My family legend has it that I am a descendent of warriors of African lands that halted the Sahara dry on its tracks. These warriors once lorded over all that is above and below the soil of the lands. The abundance of their times followed the cycle of seasons all year round. Whether within the tropics or further away towards the north or south pole, the grand pendulum of their collective existence oscillated steadily for generations.

Since time immemorial, my ancestors lived in the monotony and complacency of trans-generational opulence and satisfaction with the Gods. That was how over many days into many years my ancestors were invaded by marauding strangers from other lands beyond the Sahara. The invaders conquered my lands, enslaved my ancestors, systematically crushing their souls over time.

My ancestors hadn't seen the invaders coming. They stood no chance against the honed, effective brutality of the invaders. The invaders were already hardened, hungry, bloodthirsty battle animals conditioned by the harshness of nature and society in their original lands in the mysterious north beyond the Sahara.

My ancestors had had the inkling that beyond the Sahara were huge bodies of water in which lived big fish that fed on foolish people and animals that strayed in the waters. These awesome waters were called seas.

The seas were unimaginably bigger than the biggest rivers in my ancestors' lands. The fishes in the seas were bigger than any crocodile or snake they could have ever seen. Therefore, only the bravest and strongest of men could ever dare to cross the seas.

Moreover, to traverse the treacherously parched Sahara in any direction was a feat only achieved by few. The hardiest of men. The invasion surprise, its incomparable ruthlessness, and the awe the northerners drew from my earliest ancestors worked to the advantage of the invaders. The latter's conquest and its destructive impact on my people last to this day. Wielding economic might that's been consolidated over at least five-hundred years, descendants of invaders from the north still endeavour to attain global hegemony.

Times have changed in the 21st Century, though: I am a face amongst the not only woke but active change-makers of my generation. A new invader from the Far East is here on the scene now. They are taking the imperialistic voracity of the earlier invaders to the next level. They have learned the methods of original northern invaders well.

The northern invaders went on to ravage lands beyond the even larger sea, Atlantic Ocean, to the west of the lands of my ancestors. The former lands are called the Americas. They are divided between the north and the south not only geographically, but also according to which northern imperialist state-dominated which region over time.

North America finally fell into the hands of central and western European countries, notably England and France. Whereas South America went to southern Latin European states led by Portugal and Spain. The *Western World* describes the predominant part of the world the societies of which are run on Capitalism principles first developed by the northerners, therefore.

# CHAPTER 4

✦

# CAPITALISM
Enter China:
Africa Relations. COVID-19 Origin.

Capitalism is the economic functional mode of imperialism. The latter invades, eliminates, owns, and sustains ownership by methodical oppression of the subjugated: *veni, vidi, vici*. The former reduces imperialism bounty to numeric monetary terms. These facilitate global exchange and conveyance of goods and services through sales and purchases. That is called business.

Business is the face of capitalism. Through business acumen or sheer economic plunder, it is those capitalists with the most material bounty that rule the world.

The numeric value of monetary and material assets defines wealth, therefore. Having had the longest sustainable capitalist wealth creation in modern history, the United States of America (USA) has led and influenced western capitalists' expansion in the world. Needless to say, more often than not that with catastrophic outcomes everywhere.

With a mixed bag of good and dubious intentions, the new far-eastern invader of the lands of my ancestors is China. A perfect world scenario is that China comes into Africa to help clean up the mess created by western imperialism. However, when China applies the same business rules and treachery as the Western World in their development aid packages to Africa, then the perfect world scenario gets distorted[5]. Animosities have developed.

At the social level, extreme anti-African, anti-Black racism, Afrophobia has begun to play itself out in an appalling way in China[6].

Over the past thirty years, China has grown phenomenally into an economic force of global significance[7]. This has destabilized the balance of forces in the sphere of International Relations that had for long been dominated by the Western World with its various economic and political alliances. Included in the scenario are Russia, and, in recent times, the super-wealthy Middle Eastern oil states.

As fate would have it, the COVID-19 pandemic chose to launch its attack on humanity from Chinese soil, in the city of Wuhan[8]. It is of little interest to me as to whether or not the virus was a spontaneous occurrence, or it was insidiously created by China itself or some numerous other angels of hell as per conspiracy theories speculations.

My interest and concern are in the reality that the virus is here, and it is ravaging humanity at alarming rates and scales. Those in the living and are not yet infected by it can see its effects with their naked eyes.

Some are afraid because they fully understand the implications of the potential outcomes of the virus if measures are not taken to counteract it. They listen to information and advice given by scientists and specialist medical doctors and other relevant health workers.

---

[5]   The Atlantic, *The Next Empire*, French, HW, https://bit.ly/2EExZvN, (accessed 24 August 2020)

[6]   Mail & Guardian, *A brief history of anti-black violence in China*, Winslow, R, https://bit.ly/3hvfqJ4, (accessed 24 August 2020)

[7]   E-International Relations, *The State of China's Soft Power in 2020*, Carminati, D, https://bit.ly/3hHhKwZ, (accessed 24 August 2020)

[8]   Aljazeera, *Coronavirus outbreak in Wuhan may have started in August: Study*, https://bit.ly/32qCBxV, (seen 24 August 2020)

There are also those in the living that are indifferent. They just don't care. These may be so out of blatant ignorance or irrational belief in the power of their religious deities[9]. The deities supposedly have the control of humanity's fate in their hands: if the believers have strong enough conviction in their belief in their respective deities, the believers shall be immune from all earthly diseases, amongst other existential challenges of life on earth.

[9]   TIMESNOWNEWS.COM, *Karnataka Health Minister's 'divine intervention to fight coronavirus' comment rakes up a storm,* Hebbale, N, Author, https://bit.ly/3htJSn1, (accessed 24 August 2020)

# CHAPTER 5

# THE EQUALIZER
## COVID-19 The Indiscriminate

What objective reality shows is that all human beings are vulnerable to the invisible, deadly COVID-19. Everyone that has one way or another been exposed to the disease has been infected. The future King of England, Prince Charles, tested positive for the disease during the last week of March 2020[10].

Those that have become ill and recovered tell of horrifying bodily pains and, above all, excruciating breathing difficulties. The media is full of live documentations of ill people informing the world of the seriousness of COVID-19.

British Prime Minister, Boris Johnson, now lives to tell the story after a stint in a London hospital's Intensive Care for nearly a week. He was hospitalized on Sunday, April 05, 2020.

Boris Johnson left the hospital a humbled man one week later. It had been a close call[11].

As of Good Friday, April 10, 2020, more than 100 000 people in the world had died since the outbreak of the virus in Wuhan

---

[10] Global News, *Prince Charles breaks silence on COVID-19 battle in heartfelt video message*, Wray, M, Author, https://globalnews.ca/news/6761115/prince-charles-coronavirus-video/, (accessed 25 August 2020)

[11] BBC, Coronavirus: Boris Johnson says 'it could have gone either way', https://bbc.in/2EqaaZ4, (accessed 25 August 2020)

in December 2019. Media reports on these and the deceased's burials in various cities of the world do not make for pleasant television viewing.

On Monday, August 24, 2020, the number of reported deaths world-wide is 812 513[12]

Symptoms may or may not kick off immediately, they may or they may not be lethal, but whoever gets infected shall be a carrier of the virus to others that they come across through skin-to-skin contact. Sharing of the same immediate breathing space within a radius of 1 metre is also potentially transmissive.

The scientifically proven advice and recommendation to wash hands regularly, avoid touching of own face distinctly show that the spread of COVID-19 can be reduced and controlled until a vaccine is approved. Avoidance of touching face is important because the virus easily transmits through mouth, nose, and eyes. 1-2 metres of social distancing is another effective measure in the management of the spread of the virus.

Weren't deadly COVID-19 as rapidly infectiously prolific as it is ever so stealthy, I really wouldn't care about the outright ignorant, superstitious, and conspiracy theories adherents. I write what I write also as a means to heal my soul, and to know my world better.

I write with the humble hope that I am contributing to the pool of human thought that promotes enlightenment and reason. It is possible to align God with enlightenment and reason in our human pursuits of freedom and happiness.

---

[12] Worldometer, *COVID-19 CORONAVIRUS PANDEMIC*, DEATHS, https:// www.worldometers.info/coronavirus/, (seen 24 August 2020)

# CHAPTER 6

SCIENCE
My Philosophy

I live a life of philosophy. I am driven by science – enlightenment, and reason – concerning my tangible world with its challenges and rewards. I do not eliminate the role of subjectivity in the dynamics of provision challenges and rewards in human relations.

I am ever aware of the subjectivity of human relations dynamics even in objective contexts. Therefore, I can reason my way through the nature and attendant outcomes of my social relations. Likewise, I reason my way through natural phenomena to the extent of availability of explanatory resources and my understanding thereof at any one time.

In so far as I can reason in the face of available knowledge and my capacity to absorb and integrate it, I can predict likely future outcomes of my actions, or events in my domains. These may or may not make me happy. They may or may not infringe upon my sense of freedom.

Each time science scores a point against COVID-19 and saves more and more lives, I pray with joy and pride. My belief in humanity's capacity to find solutions to even the biggest of challenges in the material world just gets stronger and stronger. I then pray to God in gratitude for making it possible that we have amongst us those who'll have the inclination and capacity to study science and medicine, and serve and save humanity.

I turn to God for emotions that I cannot easily convey like I'd give somebody a material gift in appreciation of their service to humanity. God, my ancestral spirits, shall know how and when to reward those concerned. My out-of-this-world spiritual anchors manifest themselves in a multitude of ways to convey my gratitude to and admiration for others.

My *free spirit, have-no-fear*, and *have-nothing-to-hide* warrior ethos are a function of the omnipresence of my *out-of-this-world* spiritual anchors. I cry to them. I sing to them emotions no other human could ever understand.

They are still galactic distances away, but my writings are the nearest I can come to of expressions of the sounds that I hear from my God, my ancestral spirits. All of my deeds are nothing more than approximate expressions of wishes and instructions of the latter.

The expressions can only be approximate to allow for the interplay of the subjective aspects of my being. That is how I shall from time to time make mistakes and get burnt accordingly. If the burning doesn't kill me, that is an opportunity for my enquiring, scientific mind to grow.

Making sense of the conclusions I come to given my existence as a social entity boosts my life-driving philosophy further. The more I grow spiritually, the more my critical scientific mind grows, the more I grow as a free spirit. That way I cannot be easily swayed by half-baked, pseudo-scientists, conspiracy theorists, false prophets, and parochial religious fanatics.

And talking about false prophets and religious fanatics, I know them from afar. I am a grandson of a high priestess. My grandmother spoke with God Almighty. Our ancestral spirits guided my grandmother. Evil spirits crumbled in my grandmother's presence.

# CHAPTER 7

## DARKEST NIGHT OF FEAR
### Keep Moving!

I associate the extreme fears and attendant rational or irrational reactions to the novel Coronavirus disease (COVID-19) with lost people groping in the dark. The people are either knowledgeable and optimistic, or ignorant and nihilistic.

Growing up as a child in South Africa, the kind of extreme darkness I have experienced in tunnels and caves never frightened me much. That's because I knew that if I kept moving, I'd sooner or later meet a wall. Then I'd embrace it and keep moving along in the direction that my gut feeling told me was right. That way I should reach the end, which should hopefully be an opening to light and safety.

Sixty years ago, the darkness of the nights in Lesotho mountains used to feel tangible like a black fog. There weren't many artificial light sources glaring in the night for kilometres around then. Each time I'm on an aeroplane taking off, or descending into nimbus clouds I think of those pitch-black nights of the mountainous kingdom.

I recall one night that my guardian was teaching me how to use a torch when walking in the dark. He, *rangoane*/uncle Thuso, told me that it wasn't wise to point the torch straight into the darkness ahead or around us. He said that the darkness was so dense it was like a wall. That way, one cannot see far ahead or around because the torchlight simply blends into the darkness. The best way was to light the immediate grounds upon which we were walking.

It was nevertheless alright to point the touch ahead or around us if there indeed was a specific need or object necessitating more visibility within our vicinity. There could be sound or movement requiring further inspection, personal safety being of paramount importance here.

With more specific security considerations in mind, pointing the torch aimlessly ahead into the darkness could give away our approach to waylaying dangerous creatures or marauding individuals and gangs of the night. Or it could simply frighten others that may be feeling as insecure as ourselves.

This other one very dark night I found myself in a place that could have been anywhere in the world that I had never been to before. Although I had had no travel experience beyond South African and Lesotho borders, I had already as a four-and-half-year-old the idea that the world was a vast space beyond the two countries. I did have a sense that there was life around us. But there was nothing or nobody else to see. Absolutely.

My grandmother was there with me. Short of her holding my right hand in what I believed was her left, and hearing her voice as she talked to me, I could not make out her shape either. I had no sense of there being walls or some other objects close by to touch for us to use to navigate our way out of this horrid darkness of the night. This is what made this particular night the first truly frightening experience in my life. I have yet to endure more fright than I felt that night.

Perhaps sensing my anxiety, *Nkoko*/Grandmother said, "Are you scared, my child?"

I pulled at her hand to confirm my fear.

"What do you see around us?"

I pulled harder at her hand and stopped walking. Words failed me. I felt my body begin to tremble. Tears were just beginning to fill my eyes. My nose was also beginning to run.

"If you are only seeing darkness and nothing more, it is good. You are a big boy now. That's very good!"

I didn't know what *Nkoko* meant about me being a big boy then. But it felt good to hear. I still didn't know what to say, though. Looking back, I now understand that it was that fateful night I first became aware of any form of interpersonal communication.

With a gentle yank on my hand, *Nkoko* said, "We have to keep going, otherwise you shall get to see things that you are not supposed to see!"

We did however make a brief stop as she got me to blow my nose onto a piece of cloth. She instructed me not to cry as she wiped my eyes as well. Physically close as she was to me, I still could not see her entire physical profile. It was by her voice and body odour that I was certain that the person I was with was my *Nkoko*.

I do not recall what were the circumstances that led us to be in this strange place in the middle of the darkest of nights I had ever seen. But as we began to walk again, *Nkoko* spoke some more, "Whatever happens from now on, do not stop walking until I say so. I shall hold hard onto your hand because you mustn't let go of me; I do not want to lose you."

The situation was becoming even more confusing and frightening as *Nkoko* spoke. I thought I had finally found my voice and words to say. But as she increased her walking tempo, it took me by surprise; I tripped and almost fell.

As if reading my mind, she went on, "It's Christmas tomorrow. We have to be together with your parents and little brother. We have to get out of this place before the night is over, anyway. Otherwise, we are going to die. The spirits have revealed to me that there are people who want to kill us in the mountains here."

My parents? My little brother? I didn't know what *Nkoko* was talking about. More confusion. Up until that point, my world consisted of my grandmother alone. I had a vague picture of a man around her occasionally. He wasn't there that night.

I would later learn that that man was *Nkoko's* lover, a Mr. Machoba. He was an evil man whose violent deeds remain a talk amongst his people to this day. He had sent his agents to come and eliminate my grandmother and me that night.

"We must keep moving! Evil forces are all around us now. Hold on to me. Keep your head down. Don't open your mouth to speak to anybody else but me. If you feel anything like a person or animal getting close onto you, do not react in any way; stay as calm as you are now. Don't be afraid. Nothing will happen to you as long as you keep moving and are holding my hand. Remember, you are a big boy now. Be strong. Believe in me!"

# CHAPTER 8

# SPIRITS OF THE NIGHT
### Perseverance in Times of Uncertainty:
### Look, Listen, Query, and Learn

As the narrative continues below, significant parallels of my attitude towards the *mysteries* of the Coronavirus (COVID-19) pandemic emerge as follows:

- alertness
- curiosity
- destination
- faith
- growth
- guidance
- humility
- intuition
- resilience
- responsibility
- safety
- trust
- vulnerability

We had been walking for a while in silence when the dampened commotion I had earlier picked up around us suddenly became suppressed by an awesome sound of horses. Going by the wild shouting and whistling of men riding them, the horses were running hard. They must have been many.

I got frightened by the awareness that the horses were racing towards us from all directions. Even if I could run, I understood immediately that it would be a futile exercise.

I to no avail got a brief comfort in thinking that the wall of darkness surrounding us would stop them. *Nkoko* yanked me higher as if to lift me off the ground. At that point, I couldn't help but raise my head so that I could see these oncoming horses before they trampled us.

In an unexpected turn of events, the horses appeared as if indeed they had broken through the wall of darkness. Only that they were now charging head-on to us. Just as I thought that it was all over for *Nkoko* and me, the lead horses made an orchestrated swing to my left and continued their frenzied run passed us.

The horses were so many that it took what felt like forever before the last ones had turned their backs to us. I found that *Nkoko* and I had stood still. The suitcase she had carried on her head was now on the ground. So was the travel bag she had carried on her right hand. It had become impenetrably dark again.

From the turn she got me to make as we began to hastily walk again, I figured that we had turned around to look at the horses running towards the direction from which we had come.

Before we continued walking, *Nkoko* had remarked, "So, you what did you see?"

"Horses! Many horses. Where have they gone? Where did they come from? Did they want to kill us?"

"What else did you see?"

"I did not see their riders, even if I heard them making a lot of noise. Where are they?"

"What else did you see?"

"The horses had very long manes that almost touched the ground!"

"Anything more?"

"It became quiet as the horses ran past us. Why?"

"You will have gathered that the horses raised no dust at all. They were not touching the ground, you see. That's because they are not real. Let's go!"

"But why did they come to us? They terrified me!"

"It is the work of *baloi*/evil people that are sent to kill us. They are using magic tricks to instil fear in us so that we can separate and run in different directions. That way it shall be easier for them to do their job. It is your blood that they are after."

Images of chickens and sheep getting their throats slashed with knives crossed my mind. There was blood everywhere. I didn't know where these images came from then. It would be with time that I became aware of the fact that open slaughter of domestic birds and animals was a regular feature of life amongst my people. I may have witnessed the process before I could consciously relate to my reality.

"But I'm not a chicken, *Nkoko*! Why would anybody want my blood?"

"I shall tell you another time. You know why you must stay with me now? Your parents will kill me if I lose you here. Let us go!"

As we began to walk, I picked up another low-buzz but near enough sense of activity beside us. All this was on my left side. Somehow the impact of *Nkoko'* stating that I was a big boy fell upon me. Yes, if I were a big boy, it was just as well that whoever wanted to harm us was after me in the end. I would protect my grandmother.

To be able to protect *Nkoko*, I had to be stronger than the little boy the *baloi*/wizards thought I was. There and then I resolved that nobody shall ever slash my throat like that of a chicken or a sheep for my blood. I decided that I'd hold tighter onto *Nkoko's* hand.

Because we didn't have a torch with us, I'd keep my head high and actively look into the wall of darkness in front of us until I could see through it. I wondered if *Nkoko* saw the darkness as I did.

"I am blind as you are in these conditions, my child. This is the darkest phase of the moon we are in. Only the oldest of *baloi* are working on nights like these. It is mad people who want to die who venture out into the night now. That works to our advantage because *baloi* think I am as powerful as they are. But I'm stronger because I'm protected not only by our ancestral spirits but God also. If we survive this night, it shall be proof that you are of royalty blood indeed. That is why *baloi* of the mountains here want you."

This additional talk about dark moons, royalty blood, and God didn't make me any the wiser either. Nevertheless, the sense of importance I felt it giving me strengthened my resolve to want to protect *Nkoko*. There were also these people that were supposed to be my parents, and a younger brother I was curious to see the following day, Christmas. All this new development had come too abruptly to me. I needed time to digest it. I'd think about it until the night is over, I thought.

My thoughts were disrupted by a sudden loud noise of aggressively brawling dogs charging at high speed from behind us. They shook the ground like they were a flock of sheep I suddenly remembered seeing often passing a place I later figured out to be my guardian, *rangoane*/uncle Thuso's house. *Nkoko* stopped and turned us around to face the oncoming dogs.

"Don't move!" she hissed.

Invisible until perhaps a metre away, the leading dogs abruptly came to a halt and stiffened as if dead. The rest followed and did the same. Although I could see about three rows by five of the dogs in front of us, it was obvious that there were many, many more dogs here. *Nkoko* squeezed my hand some more. I tensed a little to assure her that I was still with her.

Then, without any warning, the dog pack snarled ferociously and in silence leaped at and past us. I could swear that I felt dog after dog passing through my body when I thought that they were attacking to bite me. When all the dogs had gone and disappeared, *Nkoko* was still by my side holding my hand.

"What did you see this time?"

"The dogs were half-bodied with no heads!"

"Again, they were not touching the ground. Another magic trick from *baloi* in this area. You kept your cool. Well done, my child. We must go before another *moleko/*trial appears!"

As we continued walking, our subtle companions had increased in numbers judging by the loudness of murmurings and sound of footsteps. I was beginning to feel their pressure on me increasing. An urge to push those nearest to me away was getting stronger every step I took. *Nkoko* jerked my hand to remind me of the need to keep calm.

My calm was broken by some wild ringing of another many, many bicycle bells coming towards us. Voices in panic kept yelling, "Out of the way, out of the way, out of the way, …!!!"

The strange feature of these voices was that they kept fading away from us the nearer the bicycles came to us. I imagined that the owners of the voices were steadily elongating backward from each of their respective bicycles. In time I would be introduced to *Chappies* bubble gums. My mind saw the screamers stretching much like the latter do when extended from the mouth by hand or some other contraption. It was an amusing visualization in terrifying moments.

"Keep moving!" *Nkoko* hissed again.

And we kept on moving. Despite the warning voices getting more and more distant, the bicycles kept getting ever more threatening in their proximity build-up towards us. *Nkoko* kept on prodding me to keep moving on ahead with her regardless.

I have no concept of how long we kept walking head-on into this impending danger. But it was so long that I began to feel weary not from the physical effort, but from the anticipation to be run over as *Nkoko* and I kept moving on ahead. Somehow the bicycles weren't breaking through the dark wall barrier surrounding us.

The fearsome invisible bicycles pandemonium finally ceased as abruptly as it had emerged. Looking around us in total bewilderment, I saw a light beam ahead of us. I could have taken it for a shooting star had it moved explosively from one point to disappear to another up in the night sky. The *mochochononol* meteorite thought reminded me of how beautiful stars of the darkest Lesotho mountain nights can be.

I found it always strange that the light of the stars never lit up the night as the moon did. The moon was so strong that the stars even gave way to it to shine as bright as it could. Except during the rains, the moon could also force clouds to open up for it much as the sun did during the day.

Pointed to the ground, this light beam I saw was moving in the opposite direction from us at an acute angle to the right. From the familiar way it was moving in an undulating manner, I figured that it was a torch in a man's hand. It had to be a man in so far as I then knew my world.

In as unpredictable fashion as all the events of the night up to that point, the light source stopped moving. After a short while, it turned, rose, and pointed directly into our direction. The total darkness around us began to ease somewhat. A bare, flat, gradually expanding landscape began to show. There were no immediate signs of people living here by way of huts or some other related structures.

This was a non-familiar territory for me. It turned to be so with *Nkoko* as well. When all of a sudden mountain-like structures began to rise from the ground some distance ahead of us, the torch turned away and continued advancing on its original path away from us. The new development within our immediate space was such that my attention soon swayed away from the torch that started it all.

I hadn't let go of *Nkoko*'s hand even for a moment all along. Looking up at her I found her gazing hard at me. For the first time since the start of all these strange events, I had a full view of her face. She looked pale. She looked different from the beautiful *Nkoko* of mine I knew. Her face looked like blood had been drawn from it.

For one moment I became overwhelmed by extreme fear not like in any way I had experienced earlier on. I wondered if the creatures of the night that had been harassing us hadn't taken over *Nkoko*'s body. Finally, I was going to die, I thought.

# CHAPTER 9

## PANIC
### The Test: *Baloi.* Prayer

In my attempt to pull away and run off, this body that I no longer felt safe with spoke with an unfamiliar soft, sobbing voice, "I'm truly afraid now, my child. These *baloi* are much stronger than I realized. If we are not careful, we shall get lost and end up falling into their trap in those hills ahead."

I cannot describe the relief I felt at knowing that I was still together with my beloved *Nkoko*. The extreme fear that had overwhelmed me got replaced by a sudden sense of strength and determination to get us out of that place. I felt it was then my responsibility to protect *Nkoko* because I never wanted to see her looking as afraid and ugly as I had just seen her. I had a feeling that she had become exhausted too. But I didn't know how I was going to go about helping *Nkoko*.

She got me back to my senses when she continued, "Come and stand in front of me. We have to speak with our *badimo/* ancestral spirits now!"

Placing her baggage on the ground beside us, she put her hands over my head. She then commenced doing a rhythmic, alternate two-step-dance on the spot, gently tapping me on my shoulders at the same time. Then she told me to close my eyes and keep my ears open.

"*Badimo* speak to us from the inside, my child. Look into your heart. It is through your heart that their voices are transmitted," she said, speaking in a detached tone of voice that I had never heard of her before. That further emphasized the gravity of the situation for me.

When she began to sing, it was in a language and a style I had never heard before. She sang as if she were many voices in one body. That made me visualize human and animal bodies of shapes and sizes I could not compare to even the oddities of the night that far.

With my eyes still closed, I felt my body expand to proportions beyond even my wildest dreams. I felt a special oneness with *Nkoko* and all these creatures that her singing brought forth into my head. A special kind of warmth and sense of peace took over my being. If I were to die, that would be the right time for it to happen, I thought.

"You may open your eyes now!" *Nkoko* spoke. Her voice was back to normal, but sounding more relaxed than she had been until then.

"*Badimo* have told me that you are their child. However, to prove your worth, they have said that you have to take us home now," she continued.

"How shall I do that, *Nkoko*?"

"Open your eyes wide and look around you. What do you see?"

"Not much except that the hills that appeared before us earlier on are no longer there. It's not bright enough for me to see everything."

"It's not what you haven't seen now that matters. What is important is what you are going to see after this: close your eyes. Take into your heart all that you have just seen, and as much as you remember of events of the night. Then, pray!"

"Pray? What is that, *Nkoko*?"

"That's a way of talking to God, child!"

"Who is God?"

"God is the maker of you and me. God is the maker of everything good and bad in the world. God helps you if you are good to other people and yourself. *Baloi* shall fail to kill us this night because God protects us. Our *badimo* have said that you stand in good stead with God. So, you have to learn how to speak with God for him to know that you know what you want. That's what prayer does. Do you understand?"

I nodded yes. This was much new information to absorb.

"Now, go down on your knees. Make a sign of the cross like this, and then pray to God and tell him what you want him to do for you. We must be gone from here before sunrise!"

I didn't know how to go about that. My eyes closed. I found myself saying repeatedly, "Please, God, take *Nkoko* and me away from here now!"

I was still asking God to take us away when I heard *Nkoko* say, "Amen!"

Opening my eyes, I found her kneeling on all fours, her arms bent at the elbows. She had her forehead into her hands. As she rose, it showed that she had been crying profusely. Wiping her tears off with a piece of cloth she had in her hands, *Nkoko* said, "You have done very well, my child. Thank you! Now, look ahead, what do you see?"

I reported that I saw a giant rock that could have fooled us to have been a small mountain had we been farther back. From where we were positioned, three footpaths emerged. One led to the left side of the rock, the second led straight towards the rock, and the third led to the right of the rock.

"Very good! You do have the eyes of *badimo*! Now, take us home. We have to move fast. The sun shall rise soon," *Nkoko* said in a now more purposeful, determined tone that did not give me a chance to say a word. She collected herself and carried our luggage like before. After I emptied my bladder as per her instructions, she grabbed my right hand again and told me to lead the way this time.

Before I could open my mouth to ask her about the path which we should take, she snarled, "Go!"

This so frightened and made me so angry that I decided I'd take any path without putting any thought to it. I just walked, pulling her as hard as I could. I had had enough of this madness. In the meantime, my right eye was twitching violently.

After a while, I had calmed down. It's by that time that I realized that in all the turmoil of emotions, I had felt a strong urge to take the path to the right side of the massive rock. A notion that perhaps that path would lead us to the place of origin of the torchlight we had seen earlier on had crossed my mind.

I somehow had the feeling that that place would be our final destination. If not, it would be a safe place to be for us to reach before we proceed on to our final destination where my parents and my younger brother were expecting us on Christmas day. The thought of meeting my unknown parents and younger brother took me to another level of the turmoil of my mind.

A special kind of happiness that I have yet to find words for engulfed me. Once again, I felt myself growing larger than life. Nothing else mattered. All that mattered then was for me and *Nkoko* to get to these three new people in my life that I felt such a strong connection with.

My mind must have switched off at some point because when I came to, I found a man and a woman listening animatedly to *Nkoko* telling them about our night adventure with *baloi* of Lesotho. I just knew that these were my parents. On my father's lap sat a big baby boy that I also understood to be my younger brother.

"You are still tired, my boy. Go back to sleep so that you are fresh and strong for Father Christmas tomorrow!" my mother spoke gently to me. I was lying next to her on a big sofa. *Nkoko* was sitting on a *moseme*/traditional straw mat whilst relaying her narrative. It felt so good to be here.

Before relapsing to sleep, the last that I heard *Nkoko* say was, "The boy is truly *ngwana wa badimo*/child of the ancestors. He is sitting on the right-hand side of God. That is how those *baloi* failed to catch him. He is protected by higher powers."

For the following years into my mid-teens, I'd be close to *Nkoko*. She has been dead for nearly twenty years now. But her spiritual influence lives on in me. On the one hand, she went on to teach me more about our ancestral spirits and God's miracles. On the other, my parents laid great emphasis on the importance of education. They insisted that educated people made for better *batho ba moya*/people of the spirits of the ancestors and God.

# CHAPTER 10

# EDUCATION
## Age of Reason Contra Conspiracy Theories

As I grew older and became more intellectually sophisticated, it made sense to me that, indeed, as my parents had drilled it into my head, educated people are trained to think as objectively as possible about life and its attributes. Further academic and professional training over time has consolidated that mental orientation.

I am trained not to take claims at face value. Before I come to my conclusions and, therefore, take a stand on issues, I must seek as much information as possible about the given subject matter. I ask relevant questions to test the logic of postulations made.

Logic lays out explanatory models of given theories about given thought systems or the occurrence of phenomena both in nature and controlled settings. Logic defines the order of intellectual and material processes leading to certain outcomes. Conversely, the occurrence of observable phenomena can be investigated to establish ascribable logical sequencing of applicable components, their nature, and the structure of processes.

Hence it is imperative that I also check out the credentials of exponents of non-conclusive, suspect, and controversial claims; call them conspiracy theories peddlers.

From findings obtained, I sort out reason from crap against available objective knowledge bases. If it is objective, it is universally infinitely repeatably tested within prescribed operational parameters to give predictably constant outcomes. This is called the scientific method of knowledge acquisition and inquiry thereof. More elegant and simpler can it not be.

The current Coronavirus disease (COVID-19) pandemic has, not surprisingly, inspired a flourishing of numerous claims that must necessarily be taken with a grain of salt: conspiracy theories. A special fascination for me regarding conspiracy theories peddlers is that they more often than not seek to crush progressive works and individuals without offering tenable alternative solutions themselves.

It is not unusual that in those untenable solutions, conspiracy theorists' own personal or group interests reign supreme; if not concerning material gains or popularity points scoring ambitions. Thanks to the exponential global growth of social media platforms. The latter continually mishmashing all sorts of information and knowledge sources to diverse audiences the world over[13].

At least in the relatively free world of western or western-oriented societies, the internet has democratized access to knowledge in ways that were near impossible to fathom only a quarter-century ago. Modern technological advances facilitate globally accessible-to information to people living even in the world's most oppressive regimes, anyhow.

---

[13] AVAAZ, *Facebook's Algorithm: A Major Threat to Public Health*, https://bit.ly/2CYks1U, (accessed 24 August 2020)

# CHAPTER 11

# LIVING KNOWLEDGE
## Internet: Age of Information

Information and Communications Technology (ICT) is the generic expression used to refer to the entire spectrum of management of information. That done through various interconnected distributive channels from source to consumption and, indeed, assessment of outcomes[14]. Conclusions derived from the assessment of outcomes will determine the overall nature of the next information loop.

This is a process that goes on infinitely, with the effect of putting ever greater pressure on ICT structures and processes, thereby stimulating constant advancements in the sophistication of information systems. The ultimate goal is to simplify and demystify complex aspects of knowledge vis-à-vis conceptual and practical human existential realities imperatives.

When the above is attained, the expectation is that the qualitative and quantitative aspects of human survival on earth shall be taken to the next level. That concerning the effectiveness and efficiency of managing life-essential means for successful existence of longevity,

---

[14] AVAAZ, *Facebook's Algorithm: A Major Threat to Public Health – Section 1 – The massive reach of global health misinformation spreading networks*, https://bit.ly/2QnE56B, (accessed 24 August 2020)

and perpetuation of the species on earth. This encapsulates the essence of societal development across the board.

There is *no-end-in-sight* in the meteoric rise of the internet and its capacity to handle gigantic volumes of data – *infinite motive circular production, capture, process, storage, distribution* – at unimaginable velocities through cable and wireless networks. Humanity is, therefore, ever so constantly barraged with information on all aspects of the human condition in the world and the wider, observable universe and beyond. That in itself ought not to be an issue because it justifiably feeds humanity's intrinsically insatiable curious nature.

The problem is imbedded in the fact that not all information incessantly encroaching upon us is useful or life-supporting. I suggest that information on its own is but a neutral tool constituting bodies of knowledge in given realms of human endeavour. Some of the elegance of modern ICT advances is that it has brought libraries, long-term custodians of human knowledge, into the home, if not at our fingertips[15].

Consequently, assuming application of the scientific method that I have already discussed above, new knowledge may be extricated, extrapolated, or insinuated more effortlessly and, thus, more rapidly than at any one point in human history. This in principle means that mankind currently lives in times when it is potentially possible to overcome challenges of all kinds of human suffering linked to inequitable access to and distribution of natural resources essential for survival on earth.

Knowledge in its pure or variably corruptible forms can then be loaded in certain information packages intended to propagate given thought patterns in time and space. The idea is to influence human behaviour in particular directions towards the attainment

---

[15] World Digital Library, *About the World Digital Library*, https://www.wdl.org/en/about/, (accessed 24 August 2020)

of predetermined outcomes by those empowered in various ways to lead, educate, or manipulate society. In politics, this is called propaganda. Whereas in business it's called marketing. In journalism, it's called news.

# CHAPTER 12

❖

# NATURE OF NEWS

News[16] may be distributed in the form of real-time events reporting. It may also be post-occurrence reporting based on actual observations of the news conveyor. That may also be enhanced by further second-hand information gathered from other sources that may have or may not have had first-hand experience relevant to the news matter. It is not unusual that news reporting may be entirely based on externally sourced volunteered or investigated information.

Investigative journalism is a more thorough, time, and resource-consuming research and analysis of specific news-making events. This is often necessitated by a need to comprehend more in-depth the circumstances that led to investigated news subject matters.

Historical, current, and, likely future components are looked into. Not in the least, the actors involved, as well as their roles and the interests they implicitly or explicitly represent personally, if not professionally or ideologically.

News is disseminated throughout the written, audio, and visual communication channels available in society: newspapers, radios, televisions, and numerous other electronic devices such as

---

[16] Lumen Learning – Boundless Political Science – *News Coverage,* https://bit.ly/3aQ2riO, (accessed 24 August 2020)

computers in various formats, as well as mobile, or smartphones. In the age of hyper-performance internet functionalities[17], the channels do now invariably have online versions.

They also exploit all the potential exposure multimedia platforms have to offer; from internet search engines like Google[18] to specialized applications like Facebook[19], Instagram[20], Reddit[21], and Twitter[22], to mention but four of numerous others the world over.

These channels will, of course, be organizationally structured to proliferate agendas of certain interest groups[23]. The interest groups will often have specific population segments they'd like to influence and appease to induce and expand loyalty.

Loyalty obtained is used to justify the existence and power of the interest groups according to each of their respective goals. It is at this point that the efficacy of news as a purveyor of objective, verifiable knowledge is decided.

*Fake news*[24] is a modern expression that is applied to the process of intentional, often maliciously calculated spread of false information about naturally occurring or artificially induced natural and societal phenomena. The general idea is to instigate and sustain scepticism, promote fear, and, in the extreme, motivate and justify rebellion against generally accepted, or mainstream knowledge bases, practices, and their proponents.

---

[17] NCTA, *THE FUTURE OF SUPER FAST INTERNET IS 10G,* https://bit.ly/3aZB3yP, (accessed 24 August 24, 2020)

[18] Google, https://www.google.com/

[19] Facebook, https://www.facebook.com/

[20] Instagram, https://www.instagram.com/

[21] Reddit, https://www.reddit.com/

[22] Twitter, https://twitter.com/

[23] AALEP, *INTEREST GROUPS AND THE MEDIA,* https://bit.ly/2FUizo0, (accessed 24 August 2020)

[24] BBC NEWS, *Fake News – What's real? What's distortion?* – https://bbc.in/3lhwsN0, *(accessed 24 August 2020)*

# CHAPTER 13

❖

# CONSPIRACY THEORIES VEHICLE
## Fake News

*Fake news* is the default communication strategy for conspiracy theories peddlers across the board. It is a disinformation, misinformation, and mal-information melting pot. As a concept, it practically takes advantage of a captive audience of millions of either like-minded bigoted and/or outright ignorant people all over the world.

Bigotry and ignorance go hand-in-hand. A dangerous, anti-human-progress combination. Ignorant bigoted types tend to exhibit one, or a combination of the following qualities:

1. A tendency to fall for verbosity and dramatics.

2. Abject laziness to make own efforts at engaging in processes of querying phenomena in society and nature.

3. Seldom willing to take responsibility for own actions: it's always someone else's fault that there are problems in the world. Therefore, reliance on prominent thought leaders in the various spheres of human endeavours for inspiration vis-à-vis beliefs and attitudes.

In this case, the charisma, the attendant achievements, and the popularity of the concerned leaders and influencers often override obvious ethical and moral considerations. All is well that is said and done by *rock stars*. An example of the biggest *rock star* in this regard may be the current president of the United States of America[25]

If the *rock stars* are unscrupulous, this category here and the one above form a crucial power base[26]. All sorts of information can be sold here. These categories are ever ready and willing to be manipulated by fake news-conspiracy theories peddlers. An extremely dangerous lot from which is recruited some of the most extreme of both right[27] – and left-wing[28] activists in world politics. The same extremism is observable in fanatical religious fundamentalism[29] the world over.

4.  A more sophisticated class of *rock stars* exhibiting some of the following qualities:
    - Arrogant.
    - Cantankerous.
    - Condescending.
    - Confident.
    - Domineering.
    - Egocentric.
    - Eloquent.

---

[25] The Atlantic – Politics – *All the President's Lies About the Coronavirus*, https://bit.ly/3j9BObp, (accessed August 24 2020)

[26] The Intercept, *ARE TRUMP AND THE ANTI-LOCKDOWN MILITIAS ITCHING FOR VIOLENCE?* https://bit.ly/2EBex31, (accessed 24 August 2020)

[27] The Guardian, *Thousands of Americans backed by rightwing donors gear up for protests*, Gabbat, A, Author, https://bit.ly/2EEwVbe, (accessed 26 August 2020)

[28] TIME, *What to Know About the Origins of 'Left' and 'Right' in Politics, From the French Revolution to the 2020 Presidential Race*, Carlisle, M, Author, https://bit.ly/3aXQXK7, (accessed 26 August 2020)

[29] Counter Extremism Project, *ISIS*, https://bit.ly/2QrfBJM, (accessed 26 August 2020)

- Exceptionally intelligent; well-informed.
- Hyperactive.
- Inclination to extremism of views held and expression thereof.
- Manipulative.
- Obstinate.
- Often high academic achievers.

Because of a high level of resourcefulness, some will be especially competent with the application of all the knowledge gathering, processing, and distribution capacity ICT has to offer[30].

This is the most disruptive of fake news and conspiracy theories peddlers' class. If allowed access into the corridors of power, they are capable of creating such tumultuous leadership scandals as to even threaten world peace.

All in all, conspiracy theories thrive on either creating fear of the unknown, or on exaggerating already existing fears of the unknown. Fear of the unknown sustains ignorance. Ignorance constructs factual falsities – intentional deceptive myths. Science mitigates ignorance.

"Focus your efforts on people who can hear evidence and think rationally", Marshall Allen[31]

---


[30] BuzzFeedNews, *These Are The Fake Experts Pushing Pseudoscience And Conspiracy Theories About The Coronavirus Pandemic*, Lytvynenko, J; Broderick, R; Silverman, C; Authors, https://bit.ly/2Qps4NY, (accessed 24 August 2020)

[31] PROPUBLICA, *"Immune to Evidence": How Dangerous Coronavirus Conspiracies Spread*, Allen, Marshall, Author, https://bit.ly/3gqfEQB, (accessed 24 August 2020)

# CHAPTER 14

❖

# SUPERIORITY OF SCIENCE

Science liberates the human spirit. Science inspires, stimulates, and facilitates inquiry, or research. Research feeds creativity. Creativity is the engine for human progress. Depending on the choices that society makes, progress can mean continual growth of knowledge acquisition and application about enduring, mutually uplifting existential relationship between humanity and nature.

Progress can also expose humanity's inadequacies against the forces of nature. It is from here that genuine forces of human progress separate themselves from the ever regressive, ignorant, superstitious, and anti-science conspiratorial ones.

For example, in times of trouble by way of natural or man-made catastrophes, the former dare to push the boundaries of knowledge to find solutions to problems arisen. Where possible, preventive measures against recurrence of the same in the future will be worked out. If recurrence arises in the future anyhow, pre-emptive systems will likely have been set in place to better manage the crises compared to previous occasions[32].

Applying scientific methods as robustly as circumstances permit, the adherents and practitioners address themselves to universally applicable principles the outcomes of which are

---

[32] DARPA, *Pandemic Prevention Platform (P3)*, Jenkins, A, Author, https://bit.ly/3gphr8h, (accessed 25 August 2020)

invariably constant within certain predetermined parameters. These will confirm previously known behaviour of matter in given situations. They also have the potential to enable the discovery of new knowledge towards improving the effectiveness of current methods and principles.

Research and Development (R & D) is the branch of science that seeks to acquire more insights as to the known generally accepted truths. Furthermore, it investigates the yet unknown vast potential of matter in our immediate and distant universes. The idea is to improve the efficacy of how society is organized: from sustainable production and distribution of food, prevention, and treatment of disease, including much more.

Society in its ever-growing complexity exerts enormous pressures concerning the planning and design of human settlements[33]. That is observable regarding sociological administration components according to prevalent modes of production in various parts of the world as well. Success here is tenable only to the extent that the scientific method and its various branches – mathematics, natural sciences (*biology, chemistry, physics*), engineering, medicine, anthropology – are applied to the highest levels a given society can afford.

Ultimately, leadership quality of the dominant classes in society shall have a bearing as to the extent of the scientific culture permeation in their respective national entities and, by extension, the global community. Science thrives and benefits humanity in relatively more open and less superstitious societies. These societies will, more often than not, be led by supportive high-calibre, progressive politicians, and other societal management forces of above-average intellectual and cultural dispositions.

The role of sophisticated, people-first, science-friendly national leadership at all levels in the various human endeavour areas is

---

[33] National Geographic, *As World's Population Booms, Will Its Resources Be Enough for Us?* Dimick, D, Author, https://on.natgeo.com/32tUsUE, (accessed 24 August 2020)

crucial for the allocation of both financial and material resources towards sustainable growth of science. Societies that invest heavily in education that emphasizes mathematics and science fare better by far in all measures of human developmental parameters[34].

In times of life-threatening crises of any kind and scale, these societies have what it takes to find solutions in time. All that assuming well-informed, grounded leadership that is capable of listening to, and acknowledging the professional and personal integrities of knowledgeable personnel charged with the problem-solving work. The latter observation has been starkly highlighted in the exceptionally successful management of the current Coronavirus disease (COVID-19) pandemic in countries as diverse as South Korea, Slovenia, New Zealand, Germany, and Norway.

In the countries above, relevant variable applications of social control quarantine and other attitudinal modification measures were set in motion. As were accompanying actual medicinal treatment regimens. All these operational strategies were largely structured upon evidence-based scientific advice from their respective national health and communicable diseases authorities.

Not in the least the WHO (World Health Organization)[35], under the auspices of the United Nations, has a global overview, advisory, and coordinating role in the governance of health and disease. Moreover, a scientifically-driven campaign to develop an anti-Coronavirus disease vaccine is being vigorously carried out by numerous key players in the field the world over[36].

Mentioning but one extreme example, The USA (United States of America) is sitting on a globally trendsetting scientific tradition

---

[34] Ingenious Science EU, *Science, technology, engineering and mathematics education – Overcoming challenges in Europe*, https://bit.ly/31sKpQB, (accessed 25 August 2020)

[35] WHO, *Coronavirus disease (COVID-19) pandemic*, https://bit.ly/2EA7M1H, (accessed 25 August 2020)

[36] National Geographic, Dozens of COVID-19 vaccines are in development. Here are the ones to follow, Mckeever, A, Author, https://on.natgeo.com/31qz8jK /,

in modern times. Unfortunately, the country is currently led by a dismally incompetent national government. This government is spearheaded by an ignorant, self-serving, delusional, myopic, anti-science-and-reason leadership. Presiding over this state is a president that daily never fails to show-case flabbergasting cognitive inadequacies.

The USA currently has the world's most stupefying numbers of positive COVID-19 cases and consequent deaths. As of Monday, August 24, 2020, the USA's Centres for Disease Control & Prevention (CDC)[37] shows 5,682,491 total confirmed cases. Reported deaths are at 196,223.

As opposed to the USA, though, South Korea[38] reports 17,665 positive cases as of Monday, August 24, 2020. Reported deaths are at 309; a mind-boggling difference.

Paradoxically, however, in as knowledge-driven contemporary Scandinavia, Sweden's[39] national leadership chose an anti-Coronavirus management path that has so far led to relatively the most catastrophic outcomes. As of August 24, 2020, the country has recorded 86,721 cases and 5,813 deaths. Whereas Norway[40] and Denmark[41] have reported 10,323 and 16,397 respectively on the same date. Deaths are 264 for the former, and 623 for the latter.

---

[37] Coronavirus Disease 2019 (COVID-19), Cases in the U.S., https://bit.ly/2CYKHoV, [accessed 25 August 2020, (*Last updated on August 24, 2020*)].

[38] Coronavirus Disease-19, Republic of Korea, Cases in Korea, http://ncov.mohw.go.kr/en, [accessed 25 May 2020 (*as of 12am on August 25, 2020, data aggregated from January 3*)].

[39] Worldometer, Coronavirus, WORLD / COUNTRIES / SWEDEN, https://bit.ly/31qX1aI, [accessed 25 May 2020 (Last updated: August 24, 2020, 22:43 GMT)].

[40] Norwegian Institute of Public Health, Daily Report and Statistics about Coronavirus and COVID-19, https://bit.ly/2Qmn7FJ, (accessed 25 August 2020).

[41] Sundhedsstyrelsen, COVID-19 up-to-date statistic in Denmark, https://bit.ly/3jhmium, (accessed 03 August 2020).

# CHAPTER 15

# CONSPIRACY THEORIES DEBUNKED

From my stories and arguments above, I hereby dismiss certain conspiracy theories assertions regarding the current pandemic with the following:

1.  The initial myth that melanin-rich people were immune to Coronavirus infection has already been crushed[42]. The fact is that the highest COVID-19 fatalities in particularly the USA and the UK are among people of African and Asian lineages. This is more out of practical living, or social conditions considerations than any uniquely specific biological pre-dispositions.

2.  Understanding of medical reports, if not medical literature in general, is not the sole prerogative of trained medical personnel. As such, there ought not to be any barriers between superrich people[43] with no medical education background collaborating with medical scientific research institutions. With relevant scientific and mathematical

---

[42]  Scientific American, *Too Many Black Americans Are Dying from COVID-19*, https://bit.ly/2QpqOKK, (accessed 25 August 2020)

[43]  CNBC, *How Bill Gates and a top doctor are pushing health care solutions in developing nations*, Barry, E, Author, https://cnb.cx/3jcndvU, (accessed 25 August 2020)

education training, people can read and understand all sorts of texts written in familiar languages[44].

3.  Applied Mathematics models have sent people to the moon and back[45]. Space travel is a direct function of mathematical modelling processes underpinning all aspects of physics, chemistry, and biology involved in the endeavour. Modern algorithmic Big Data[46] analytical methods propelled by Artificial Intelligence (AI)[47] are used to, amongst others, analyse given trends in all areas of human endeavour. From this, some appreciable degree of understanding of why, how, and when certain events occur may be acquired. Needless to say, AI is anchored in mathematical principles.

Thus, predictions of future outcomes can be made from the scientific knowledge gathered. Any enlightened person ought to know that it's the easiest exercise for an enthusiastic billionaire IT genius to predict with a high level of probability when and how a viral disease pandemic will break out.

There is no evidence that the COVID-19 pandemic arose from predictions made by some mentally deranged IT billionaire genius[48]. They simply *saw* it coming. All that

---

[44]  Inc., *3 Things a Book on the 1918 Flu Taught Bill Gates About Leading During a Pandemic*, Stillman, J, https://bit.ly/34sXlI6, (accessed 25 August 2020)

[45]  NASA, Math Invented for Moon Landing Helps Your Flight Arrive on Time, Tabor, A, Author, https://go.nasa.gov/31xFn5v, (accessed 25 August 2020)

[46]  Guru99, *What is BIG DATA? Introduction, Types, Characteristics & Example*, https://bit.ly/32whpqy, (accessed 25 August 2020)

[47]  Britannica, *Artificial intelligence*, Copeland, BJ, https://bit.ly/2FYnlRp, (accessed 25 August 2020)

[48]  The Mercury News, *Coronavirus: Bill Gates predicted pandemic in 2015*, Rogers, P, Author, https://bayareane.ws/34BPHLt, (accessed 25 August 2020)

based on revelations by outcomes derived from testable extrapolatory scientific research methods applied.

Predictions were thus made so that the powers that be in the world should be prepared for the eventuality: design and apply sustainable pre-emptive, containment, treatment, and ultimate control, if not total elimination of the pandemic.

If an IT genius of the stated calibre intends to eliminate certain high fertility groups of people as a way to curtail human population growth on earth, they sure are capable of effecting that relatively at a fraction of time and cost involved.

To first engineer an ultra-contagious disease, develop a fatal vaccine, and then go out and inject millions of people to death all over the world is an utterly cumbersome, nonsensical economically non-viable venture.

4. The investment costs of developing pioneering medicines and vaccines are astronomical. Philanthropists with interest and means to support should be encouraged to do so within provisions of local and international laws. If they don't, who will? Certainly not some petty, incompetently ignorant psychopathic political leaders of some of the economic and scientific cutting-edge nations of the world.

It's preposterous to suggest that these high-profile global philanthropists are in it only for the potentially high returns on their investments. But of course, profits are essential if the work shall be sustained over time. Some of these big philanthropists are, in the first place, so wealthy that what they contribute to these projects is but a drop in the ocean for them.

5. There are more practical and more cost-effective ways of eliminating people from the face of the earth than with some stupid vaccines that take forever to develop and are much trouble to administer and manage.

It goes against capitalist common sense thinking to assert that some billionaire *fake* philanthropists are out there conniving with some unethical scientists to develop vaccines and other medicines to annihilate the population of Africa. Every enlightened capitalist knows that Africa is the most exciting consumer and industrial market of the future[49].

The major factor that threatens the future of Africans and other Black people of the world is ignorance and the resultant fear of the unknown. That notwithstanding, it is an observable phenomenon, as I have illustrated earlier on in the text, that ignorance and fear of the unknown are not race-specific. They are common human traits. That is how well-spun conspiracy theories or marketing campaigns can have huge global impacts. They cut across race, colour, creed, gender, and such other artificial social segregation categorization.

The core element here is to play on people's emotions above all else: plant, enhance ideas of suspicion and hate for strangers; the super-rich want to own the world and turn everyone else into their slave robots; extra-terrestrial forces are using certain interest groups, i.e. business, political, and cultural elites, to eliminate humanity through spreading incurable diseases and the like.

I stand free with the confidence that Coronavirus disease shall eventually be understood. With the current intensive global scientific research and vaccination development effort going on,

---

[49] IFC, *SHAPING THE FUTURE OF AFRICA – Markets and Opportunities for Private Investors*, https://bit.ly/2QmTNyD, (Accessed 25 August 2020)

it's only a matter of time before a workable treatment solution shall be found. There is no need to worry. No need to panic.

So that safety and qualitative standards are met, necessary timelines have to be adhered to in the process. Concerned scientists know better. In the meantime, I shall relate myself to expert medical advice because universally applicable practical preventive measures have been established:

1. Avoid touching the face.

2. Be aware of the symptoms.

3. Do your necessary work assignments. Read, write. Keep oneself updated on current affairs. Stay well-informed.

4. Exercise. Eat well. Drink water adequately. Have enough sleep.

5. Ignore irresponsible antics exhibited by certain prominent world leaders.

6. Ignore the noise made by garrulous, petty, attention-seeker conspiracy theories peddlers across social media platforms.

7. Practice 1–2 metres apart social distancing.

8. Stay at home. Respect quarantine regulations.

9. Stay strong, and help others as necessary.

10. Take care of family and social relations: electronic communication.

11. Test, and seek medical attention as necessary.

12. Use hand sanitizer.

13. Wash hands regularly.

14. Wear a face mask in public spaces, especially in supermarkets and public transport facilities.

For as long as I remain alive, for as long as my cognitive functions remain as sharp as they currently are, I cannot be easily carried away by any theories that lack conventional scientific precepts. At the subjective level, any postulates that do not satisfy my existing philosophical inquiry assumptions cannot excite me either.

The least a subjective postulate can do is to arouse my curiosity to seek more relevant knowledge for me to come to a better-informed conclusion. I am not inclined to exerting energy on claims that from the outset sound non-sensical to me.

I conclude, therefore, that Coronavirus disease (COVID-19) is here, and it is as real as can be. As to who started it, where, and why are for me not as important as finding the cure as scientifically and as defensibly rapid as possible.

The fact is that an active Coronavirus disease infection can be fatal if it is not checked in time, treated effectively, and the patient does not respond accordingly. It doesn't matter who the patient is, or where the patient comes from.

Once it has struck, COVID-19 kills both the sceptic and the scientist or medical personnel alike. For now, the disease cannot be cured by chance, speculative medicine like the established anti-malarial hydroxychloroquine[50].

The disease must fear the future. Science shall conquer for sure. No hysterics. We shall beat this. Until the scourge is overcome, listen to expert scientific advice. Follow the guidance of progressive, informed local, multilateral organizations, and national leaderships. The future is ever so bright when science and sober minds rule.

(END: 25/08-2020)

---

[50] Scientific American, *Nine COVID-19 Myths That Just Won't Go Away*, Lewis, T, Author, https://bit.ly/2QpVtru, (accessed 25 August 2020)

# BOOK 2

❖

# BLOG ARTICLE

# CHAPTER 16

# SHOULD I DIE
COVID-19 Reflections

In 1998, my father died solitary in a bachelor quarter in Tshwane, South Africa. My mother followed twenty years later. Pneumonia related complications in both cases.

There were about eleven other fellow patients in my mother's ward at the hospital in Thabong, Welkom. She had kept everyone awake all night with her moaning in pain, crying out an unknown name all along. Nevertheless, she managed to eat her 0700RS breakfast that fateful Sunday morning; much to everyone's delight since she hadn't had much appetite the two previous days. After eating she fell asleep.

When my nephew, Kgosi, and I went to check on her during the morning visit hour between 1000-1100HRS, we found her sleeping peacefully. Apparently. After hearing the report by fellow patients about my mother's restless night, we thought it wise not to immediately awaken her. She could have her full sleep during the morning, and we'd come back to see her again in the afternoon as per routine.

Fifteen minutes into our arrival in the ward, an impatient family friend found that my mother was cold and lifeless. A few minutes later, a doctor declared her officially dead. She had probably died two hours earlier. No one had taken notice. It was one of those cases of "She died peacefully in her sleep", I guess. Perhaps the same may be said about my father. He had been dead for about two days by the time his corpse was found in his residence.

I opt to convince myself that, indeed, both my parents died peacefully in their sleep when their respective times to go arrived. Neither was surrounded by their loved ones upon breathing their respective lasts.

The thought of whether or not my death will pounce on me in solitude has been on my mind since February 1991. I had for the first time taken ill with what I later understood to have been an acute attack of the flu. Bedridden with high fever and profuse sweating for three days in my single student room, I was so weak that I was unable to lift a telephone sitting beside me on my bed to call my school or doctor in Oslo.

One week later I had recovered without having had received any medical attention. An older, more knowledgeable friend told me that I had had a close brush with death. Perhaps I should consider getting myself a wife, he suggested. He argued that many people who live alone tend to die unnecessarily because there is often nobody there to render immediate assistance in times of emergencies.

In the northern hemisphere spring of 1995, I had a first-time mean attack of hay fever. I didn't know what it was at first. For many days I kept sneezing like what I thought was like a mad man. Then I began to cough as inexplicably madly. What I thought sounded like a small cat soon started mewing in my chest. This made breathing painfully difficult even at the mildest physical exertion. Then I knew I was in trouble.

At a great financial cost to me that I could afford regardless, a former lover at that time then finally hastily made it possible for me to acquire an emergency cocktail of various tablets, capsules, and an assortment of asthma medicines. Had I been alone at that critical time, I could have died from pneumonia, the former lover said later.

Today, the Coronavirus disease (COVID-19) pandemic, moving at a frighteningly fast pace is threatening human life across the globe. The United Nations and national governments are taking drastic and, in some cases, Human Rights defying draconian measures in individual and concerted efforts to isolate, treat, control, and eventually effectively manage the disease.

The ideal situation would be to eliminate the disease, of course. But it'll take time to develop and subsequently approve necessary relevant curative and preventive medicine. Researchers the world over are currently working at break-neck speeds to achieve the latter.

Millions of people are under various levels of quarantine throughout the world, depending on suspected or actual infections and severity. Much of the industrialized world is under lockdowns.

People whose immune systems are compromised from before are dying rapidly. Some people are quarantined in their private homes with their near family units. I am alone in my abode.

I am feeling well and strong. I can't help, though, but think about my mortality if my health should take a sudden, COVID-19 related downturn. Some other shit could happen too. One never knows when shit will hit the fan.

I can't help but think that were I to die now, I sure would do so peacefully. I'd die with no beloveds of mine surrounding me. If it happened to my parents, it might as well be the same with me. Family solidarity. Family tradition. I'm their eldest child after all.

Like my parents, I'd leave no great fortunes behind. It's just as well for me that, unlike my parents, I'd leave no children behind. As to whether or not it's a good thing to die as my corpse shall be in a cremation oven, I shall find out upon arrival on the other side.

In the meantime, I can't help thinking about one of my all-time favourite songs: *If I Should Die Tonight*, by Marvin Gaye. I've loved this song ever since the release of the *Let's Get it On* album in 1973. The album title hit song planted me to its moment and has stuck with me to this day. However, *If I Should Die Tonight* continues to throw me back to a period that I now know marked the closing chapter of the happiest times of my childhood years: the close of the 1960s decade to much of 1970.

I got honey-sweet infatuated with an older woman during this time. She remains one of the most beautiful women I have ever seen.

This woman was the mother of my puppy love object at that time. And she was heart-warmingly kind to me. This woman had the sweetest of sweet singing voices. She, together with some of her male contemporaries in our neighbourhood, used to sing acapellas of popular soul hits of the time: *When a Man Loves a Woman*, *Crying Time*, *Stand By Me*, and many more.

The sweetness that the whole of my being feels at the thoughts of this woman is one of the sources of my emotional and spiritual strength at any time. This sweetness constantly fuels my desire to live and to love for as long as my life and capacity to love shall last. For I live, for I love, I shall dream, I shall hope, I shall create. For I create, I shall live forever.

I don't have to meet the perfect woman for a lover. It's not necessary. It's not important for me at the stage of life that I have now reached. I don't need to.

But this *If I Should Die Tonight* lady is one of those women that have profoundly impacted my life. That to such an extent that I pin on memories of her my belief that a perfect woman for a man is found somewhere out there in the wide, wide world. It's only a question of whether the mortal man shall live long enough, shall travel the world wide enough. Even then, like the song says, "… If I should die tonight, though it be far before my time, I won't die blue 'cause I've known [her] …"

There is much more to the phrase *I won't die blue* for me. I won't die blue. Never. I'll die a contented man should I die at this very moment. It's a daily preoccupation of mine to seek to do all that is within my powers to prolong my longevity for as long as it is possible. If I have a pre-determined lifespan, I want to beat it. Should I, however, die at this very moment, I'll die a well-pleased man knowing that I have defied death several times before.

I'm convinced that I have lived way past my allotted lifespan. But this I can only confirm to be true or false upon my getting onto the other side. If all truths of my life are indeed found on the other side, I certainly will be a happy man should I die now: finally, I shall get to confirm who I really am, what my real purpose in life on earth was.

Until then, within the best of my cognitive potential performance, given limitations of my human existential imperatives vis-à-vis universal creation, the following is the consciousness I'll be taking with me should I die now:

- For all their strengths and their vulnerabilities, I got the best parents that I deserved. I would choose them again could I start all over again. Even in death, I love my parents very much, with all of my heart; I admire them beyond words. The joys of their lives I never think too much about. Joy never bothers me at all.

  I take it for granted that life ought to be a joy. Pure joy. Have joy, no worries. But I feel the pains of my parents' lives from their beginnings to their ends.

  Against the toughest odds, my parents managed to nurture the life that they had given me. They gave me all they could according to their life circumstances as a couple, and as individuals in a hard world. They had to endure untold sufferings, make huge sacrifices for that I could breathe, and subsequently have the power to carve my own spaces of manifestations of my influence through my creativity on planet earth.

If my creative power influence manifestations transcend planetary boundaries into the farthest realms of the universe, it is owing to, in search of, and for my parents on the other side. I want to tell them that I'm a humble but proud symbol of that they, indeed, left this world a better place than they found it. Thank you very much!

In all my endeavours, I am heavily inspired by my parents. It is in their honour that I do the good that I am often told that I do. It is for me and me alone to take the heat for the bad that I do.

The bad that I do is never representative of the upbringing that my parents gave me. The errors I commit from time to time are a reflection of my failings, my stupidity embedded in my inherent human imperfections.

My parents are not my everything. My parents are but a microcosm of the grandeur of being human in the face of creation's stupendous infinite spectrum of possibilities with all that humanity knows and has yet to fathom about it.

I'm not an emulation of my parents. I'm but an extension of their joint and individual life forces. In that regard, creation dealt me a hand that is my own to play from birth. That in line with how I could synchronize with my parents' energy bundles influences in me. Also, according to how optimally I could utilize the unique powerhouse that I am in my journey through the infinitely intricate maze that is life.

I hope that as they took their last exhalations, my parents knew in their respective lonesome moments of dying that I hadn't done half of what I had wished to do for them in appreciation of their having brought me to life and all the good that they ever did for me.

Furthermore, I hope that they knew that whatever little I did to make them happy were outcomes of only the best that I could do, having given only all the best effort I could harness for the goal when it mattered.

Consequently, I won't die blue if I should die tonight because my heart is at peace concerning my parents' lives and how in their way, they have contributed to making this world a better place than they found it from the times they were born.

My parents never got to see their grandchildren from me. Were children made like bread, I'd have produced one-thousand-and-one-plus grandchildren for them. With the power of the written word, though, my parents' legacies are etched in words by their thousands in thousands of pages in books that I have already written, and those that I have yet to write.

Children might be born, die, and be forgotten. Books might be written, get destroyed, and burned, but words are eternal. Mr & Mrs. ELWLM Chilembo, you have been immortalized. Now I can die.

- No, I won't die blue if should I die this moment. I won't die blue should I breathe my last tonight. I'll be by myself. No one making noise around me, delaying my dying process. Should I die now, it'll be peaceful. Really. I won't be blue.

  I might see shades of blue because I'll take my death like it's an invitation into a meditative trance. I'll spread my wings to fill up the entire blue sky for a moment, bid farewell to planet earth, and then merge with the vastness of space beyond.

  Before I disappear into outer space forever, I'll reach out to all those earthly souls that gave me so much joy, so much love in the living. They'll say they saw me in their dreams. It is for these people that I have no fear of death.

  These loving souls ever gave me so much more than I could ever ask for their kindness and generousity. It is for these people that if I should die tonight, it'll be because my time to die would have arrived for sure.

Just like my parents, I'm no more than a microcosm of the grandeur of life. The good that I do is also grounded in the love, support, understanding, and tolerance of all the wonderful people with whom I've had the privilege of interacting in my life. It is for these people that I won't die before it is my time.

- I won't die blue were death to take me away tonight because I know that I never set out to make this world a worse place than I found it. Although I'll be dying knowing that, also here, I never achieved half of what I had dreamed of doing for the world, I gave the best that I could, given the opportunities accessible to me and my strength to work.

- With time, the illumination that I could only be that which I am here and now, and I could only do what I do in a given time and space, freed my soul. I understood that I could only allow myself to be taught, led, and inspired by others.

But I could never replicate them and their deeds. Neither could I necessarily ever replicate external manifestations of their successes, if not their abilities to shape even global trends across the entire sphere of human endeavour. This was that moment of *know thyself* landing home at last.

By extension, it became clear that I also could only teach, lead, and inspire. It's never a given that all my protégés will share my values and social skills in the end. As such, I won't die blue should I die this moment because I know that as much as I am loved, I am loathed in certain quarters.

The choice to love or loathe is a personal prerogative based on certain reasons only known to the lover or loather. If these reasons ever are revealed, they do not have to make sense to the loved or loathed.

I know that if I should die tonight, I'll die with a smile on my face because I'm so full of love. I know that if I should die tonight, I'll die with peace because I know that I've had all the fun I could reach for and accommodate in my life. May haters have a good life.

May Coronavirus disease (COVID-19) die tonight. Perhaps not. COVID-19 knows no lovers, no haters, no irrational human segregation rules. If the virus stays just a little longer, humanity might, at last, learn that we can make this world a far better place if we all understood that we are all equally small and vulnerable against forces of nature.

COVID-19 shakes even the foundations of both the concept of God and her might. Many an oppressor, a racist of the world has God as their spiritual and purported racial superiority anchor. If COVID-19 destabilizes even the almighty God's multifaceted global movement, it goes to show that forces of evil seeking to destroy the good of humanity have no future. COVID-19 may be but a small pre-taste of hell.

Another Soul singer, Curtis Mayfield, has said: *If There's a Hell Below We're All Going to Go.* We might as well all be humane towards one another as all one, same universal person. But then again, this kind of talk is beyond the cognitive capacities of propagators of racism and oppression in the world today. Ignorant fools. Stupid idiots. Psychopaths. It is these scum that COVID-19 must rid of the face of the earth.

SIMON CHILEMBO
OSLO
NORWAY/March 15–16, 2020
Blog – https://wp.me/pBoMW-159

BOOK 3

❖

**COVID-19 POEMS**

# CHAPTER 17

⊰⊱

# THE UNTHINKABLE – 1

The unthinkable happens
When it happens
And we pay the price
It's simple
To kill
One hundred thousand people
In a spring of
One year

**Move slow**
Like a ship
Sinking in icy waters

**Be stupid:**
*No, the ship won't perish*
*Water shall freeze*
*It shall keep the vessel together*
*Iced machines don't move, see*

*We're doing great*
*Great job*
*We won't drown*

*Maybe summer will come*
*Maybe it won't*
*We'll see what happens*
*You never know*

*And, yes,*
*Maybe ice shall turn into water again*
*Maybe it won't*
*Who knows*
*We see what happens*

*All we got to do is*
*Move on with our sailing*
*We were made to sail*
*The world over as we want*
*We are the greatest people ever*
*In the history of mankind*
*It's our right*
*We deserve it*
*I won the election*
*It was perfect*
*Perfect like*
*The letter*
*The call to Ukraine*
*You know*
*Perfect like never before*

**Don't be sorry:**
When
The unthinkable happens
The sea thaws in silence

Ferocious as a tornado
In a silent movie
It swallows down the ship
A hundred thousand people die
Right in front of your eyes
But this is fake reality to you

For each dead person
A hundred thousand pairs of eyes cry
They shed tears
Enough to raise the sea level by
A hundred thousand millimetres
A hundred thousand more
People are going to die
We are all going to perish

Your eyes are dry
You are so stupid
Your brains are so dry-iced
You don't know
How to cry

Your brains cannot see
That
The solution is
Noah's ark
The drawings are here
So are the engineers
There is a bit of time yet
Teach people how to swim
Build boats
Train sailors

Your brains are so dry-iced
Your hearing capacity
Is impaired
You cannot listen to reason
When you speak
Your speech spews
Sounds of cracking
Contaminated
Dry-ice that forms your brain

Coronavirus disease
Covid-19 is here, see
It arrived well and safe
It didn't disappear
Its miracle is in its
Contamination potency
In the same fashion as are your words

You say bad things
You say wrong things
You do just
The right kind of vile things
To contaminate the atmosphere
For Covid-19 to ravage
One hundred thousand people
In gratitude
This spring

You know how they died
Covid-19 denies people air to breathe
Just like water does in drowning

You are a ship's captain
The unthinkable
In your imbecilic mind
Has happened

Some people
Hear your words
Do what you say
They die

Other people
Hear your words
See your actions
Do what you do
They die

You wear people down
People lose hope
The nightmare
That you are
Horrifies people to death

You have blood in your hands
Does that even make any sense to you at all
An unthinkable tragedy
That you are
Must never be allowed to happen again

END
©Simon Chilembo, 01/05-2020

**NB:**

- Deadliest day, USA – https://www.cnbc.com/2020/05/02/who-us-just-reported-deadliest-day-for-coronavirus.html (Total, 02/05-2020: 65,173)

- See also: "US coronavirus death toll surpasses 100,000," https://youtu.be/CVLpAMlaoM8 (CNN, accessed 27 May 2020)

- USA tragedy continues. As per Saturday afternoon CET (Central European Time), July 18, 2020, numbers stand as follows*:
  i)  Coronavirus Cases: 3,770,012
  ii) Deaths arising: 142,064

***Worldometer** (real time) – https://www.worldometers.info/ and **nCoV2019.live** (real time) – https://ncov2019.live/data

# CHAPTER 18

# RIPE OLD AGE – 1

*O hole o khokhobe*
Grow into
A ripe old age
May you grow so old
You crawl on your belly
For walking
Basotho people still
Say it today

There was a time
Aging was an honour
There was a time
Ripe old age
Was a blessing
All able hands
There for you
Feeding on the warmth
Of your frail body
Their ears
Feeding on the wisdom of
Your last words
Their eyes

Drowning in
Floods of tears
Watching
You die so slowly
You are indifferent
To any thread of life
Dangled for you to
Hang in there
Please
Grand one

The English say
Happy birthday
They mean well
But
My birthday 2020
Googles my eyes
Straight onto
The face of death
Coming onto me
So fast
I'll die like an
Unripe fruit falling
Off a tree
During a hail storm
Ripe old age
Is a curse
These days

In Norway
They say
Congratulations on your day

When they want
To say your birth date

I hang onto
My birthdate
With a prayer
That I shall wake up tomorrow
To find that it'll have morphed
Into a key
Into the house of
The elixir of youth
Only with that
Can I celebrate
And be grateful for
My birthdate 2020
And the birthdates beyond

They have made Coronavirus disease
Cull the old
They say the world is not enough
Let the unborn stay wherever they are
They call it population control

Let youth in the middle stay
They can tolerate high fevers
Every now and then
One or two might die
That's okay
Afterall
One of them has said it before
In the
*Uneducated* States of America

"If I get corona, I get corona!"
They're all gonna get old anyway

COVID-19 sounds like
It's a name for
Cannibals' highway to hell
Beckoning for the
Ripe old age
Generation
I refuse to go
I have lost my birthdate
I remain forever young

END
©Simon Chilembo, 13/05-2020

# CHAPTER 19

# SEA OF POSSIBILITIES – 1

My guru told me
That
It is in the nature
Of the mantra to disappear
Mantras have strong wills
Of their own
You see

Whether
The mantra
Runs away
Or simply just
Walks away
Or it flies away
Maybe
Or just
Vanishes into thin air
Or the storm of your emotions
Blows it away
It is not a matter of concern
For you
My guru said

Just chant the mantra
It will come back
Or you will find it again

You might lose yourself
Disappear from everything
Including your mantra

Mutual disappearing
And self-rediscovery
Is the nature
Of your
Relationship with
Your mantra

I got lost from
My mantra
I found myself
Counting my steps
Kinhin meditation style

I had been walking
Around Oslo
For one-eighth of a day

My feet were sore
The pain incomparable
To that in my heart
Though

What if
The solitude
Of the city

Midnight hours
I had walked through
In the past eight weeks
Were to last
Eight months
Eight years
Eight decades
Would
Eight centuries
Of Coronavirus disease
Human life extinction matter

It was time
To sit down
Or I' die
Away from my mantra

My eyes opened
To find that
I was on a bridge
Over an Oslo city harbour
Suburb canal

Calm of the sea
Mellowed my sense of solitude
Thoughts of life underwater
Soothed my body pains
Full moonlight
Multicoloured city lights
Dancing with ripples on
Seawater' surface
Shone to me faces
Of all humanity

Yonder
The moon reflected in full
I closed my eyes
I inhaled
I held my breath
I exhaled
My eyes opened
To find the face of
My guru
Rising from
The shape of the
Moon in the waters
It had been
Half of
Eight decades
Since I last saw him
Since I last heard his voice

He gave me
My new mantra
With that he said
I'd grasp the extent of
Humanity's survival
Possibilities in the
Post-COVID-19 hibernation epoch:
Count the number of
Ripples on the waters
Count until
The numbers disappear
From your consciousness

Recover the numbers eight times
Do this eight times to

The power of eight
When the numbers think
They have worn you out
Repeat eight times
To
The power of eight
Eight times
To
The power of eight
And repeat

The pandemic
Cannot exterminate us
Our spirit is infinite
Like seawater ripples

END
©Simon Chilembo, 16/05-2020

# CHAPTER 20

# FEAR NO DARKNESS

I can endure the dark
I just close my eyes
And zoom out to the stars

I do not fear the dark
For stars rule
Skies of the night
Dark as they want to be

They say stars shine
Beyond themselves

I may be imprisoned
In a black hole
Of uncertainty
In Coronavirus disease
Pandemic times
But my star lights
Transcend
Fears of the unknown
Lies about the unknown

The dark come and go
But
Starlights endure
When tired
They mutate
Multiply
And
Live forever

END
©Simon Chilembo, 19/05-2020

# CHAPTER 21

## FREEDOM
### To Die or Not to Die For

When I'm dead
I'm dead

Me dead
My life
As I lived it
The joys
It gave me
The sweet life
Of
Wines and roses

The trials and tribulations
It subjected me to
The sour life
Of
Swords and sores
Don't matter no more

Heaven and hell
Are

Illusions
For
The afterlife

Therefore
In the living
I worry
But little about them

I have
This vision
That
I shall die as I lived
A spirit
Hooked on freedom

Freedom taught me that
It is like the air
It is love

Love is the
Axis
Around which
The earth rotates

Without air
I can't breathe

I can't breathe
I die

I die
Earth axis vanishes

All love lost
Earth rotation stops
All hell breaks loose

Deprivation
Of freedom
Strangles me
Constricts my lungs
Inflames my sinuses

I can't breathe?
I don't die?
I panic
I go berserk

I go berserk
I feel no pain
Fear evaporates from my body
I am mad
Like a
*Médecin sans frontières*

Deprivation
Of freedom
Makes the
Line between life and death
Very thin
Every which way
I'm heard
I'm seen
If I die
I do so
For the living

To breathe
They'll call my action
The ultimate sacrifice

If I live
I won't celebrate
Until
I can shout out
Freedom
From the depth of my lungs
I'll call that pure joy

In the name of freedom
A man defied
Military tanks in
Tiananmen Square

In the name of freedom
Somebody is
Incarcerated in
Dark holes every day
Claustrophobic
No food
Nor drink
Worth talking about

They'll tell you about
Robben Island
In the
Land of my birth

I can't breathe

In the name of freedom
Somebody takes
A bullet in the head every day

In the name of freedom
People of the world
Turn
Blind eyes to
Coronavirus disease
COVID-19
Conveniently called
The invisible enemy

That is
The price of freedom

Let us breathe
Give us our lives back
Nothing
No one can stop us now

We need to breathe
Whatever the cost
No freedom
No rationality
It is what it is
If I die, I die
I won't be the first
To die
In the name of freedom

END
©Simon Chilembo, 07/06-2020

Dedicated to anti-racist protests world-wide. George Floyd's murder legacy is larger than life. Change has to happen. Freedom sure does not come cheap.

**NB:** I do not trivialize the seriousness of Coronavirusdisease (COVID-19) with this piece of writing. The pandemic deserves the highest respect: we must all follow expert advice from doctors, scientists, and relevant multilateral and state health authorities wherever we are in the world.

# CHAPTER 22

❖

# FALSIFIED
## I Keep on Penning

So
I
With pure heart
Write books
People misunderstand me
They wish me dead

Powers that be
Gag me
I cover my mouth
They think they got me
COVID-19 got me thinking
We've got a good thing going here

So
I write more books
If I die I die
If I breathe
They can't stop me

I die
When I die
Ain't over
'til I'm over
This is my life
I make the rules
Ain't for nothing
That
I'm
Machona Son

So
What you gonna do
Now

END
©Simon Chilembo, 23/07-2020

# CHAPTER 23

## THE THRESHOLD

I keep wishing against wish
That I won't be here
When the big bells gong
Two hundred thousand times
    Not marking
    The
    Two hundred-thousandth hour
    But commemorating American person
    Number two hundred thousand
    To die from COVID-19
    In the fall of year
    Two thousand and twenty

It had been unthinkable
That it could happen
But the first
One hundred thousand Americans
Fell to the pandemic
In the spring of the year
Two thousand and twenty

They never saw
New life bloom
For the season

I cried an ocean
Into the summer
Where I saw people of the world
Storm the streets
Defying COVID-19
Crying that
*Black Lives Matter*
After
American George Floyd
Barely managed to
Squeeze out the phrase of despair
*I can't breathe*
As he slowly died
Under fellow American policeman's
Knee on his neck

I hope that
Those'll be the final gongs
And then the bells
Shall finally drop
Crash to
Two hundred thousand pieces
On the ground
And die
Forever

Should I hear
The
Two hundred thousand-and-first gong

Then I'll cry to God
To tell her that
I can't take this anymore
Please let me die too

I no longer know
How to comfort the living
Hope has lost meaning
People say that
Death is no longer
That mysterious inevitable
That God plays on us
Like we do with our puppets on strings

These days we glare into death's eyes
Coming straight on to us
Like high-speed trains

We are all chained
Onto rail tracks of the world

And somebody in America says that
We might
We might not
Die
    The train might
    Or might not decimate us
The train will just disappear
We'll see what happens
    We're doing great
    The economy is good
    Wall Street is happy

People die
It is what it is

Well
I see debris
Of fallen walls
Strewn all over the street
This place resembles a war zone
9/11 pictures
Are still fresh in mind
It'll be twenty years since
Next year
I'd have thought that
The world would be
A better place today

Mortuaries over-flowing
In New York
They stashed corpses
In trucks[51]
In the sun
President
*The Belligerent*
Has lost the plot

I see the
Charging Bull
Lustreless
On the knees
The horns are broken

---

[51] The New York Times, *Dozens of Decomposing Bodies Found in Trucks at Brooklyn Funeral Home,* https://nyti.ms/2YA5N4n, (accessed 20 August 2020)

Body orifices bleeding
The beast is dying slowly
Somebody must have fed it
Shredded metal pieces
Thinking that it'll
Defecate
The mighty greenback

Bulls die
No *torero* in sight
People die
It is what it is

I keep telling myself that
I shall wake up
To find that it all
Had been a nightmare
Of global proportions

We had all been 5G'd
In our brains already running
Wild on
Psychedelic mushrooms cocktails
Injected into
Our 21st Century Super Foods
Spiked into our health drinks
They call them nutraceuticals
Of the times

And then we saw things
In the land of the free
We fantasised people dying
By their tens

By their scores
By their hundreds
Their thousands
Their tens of thousands
In the home of the brave

Now people are dying
In the hundreds-of-thousands magnitudes
I don't want to be here
They say that
Come wintertime
Three hundred and nine thousand nine hundred and eighteen
Americans
Will have perished[52]

The truth is
That's reality
To see
To smell
To touch
    The dead don't speak
    The dead don't seek jobs
    They don't strut
    Beauty pageant stages of the world
    It's not a TV show
    No fake news

We live in scary times
When our salvation

---

[52] IHME COVID-19 Projections: United States of America, https://bit.ly/2EpzrCE, (accessed 22 August 2020)

As the human race on planet earth
Is clearly in our hands

Wash the hands clean
Keep your hands to yourself
Use your hands to
Help you to breathe
Uncontaminated air

Put on a mask

Use your hands to
Define your safety spaces
Use your hands to
Reach out and find
Good books to read

Use your hands to
Dig wells of knowledge
To nourish your head with
Science of the world
For its elegance
Its barbarity

Use your hands to
Hang onto the good of science
Use your hands to
Wash your face
To open your eyes to
To allow your brains to see
Common sense in
How to be human amongst other humans

If you are too blind to see
Use your hands to
Unplug your ears
And listen to those that know
How the world works
*From the point of view of science*

You are a lost cause
You are beyond redemption
The blood of
Two hundred thousand people
Dead needlessly
Dead in vain
For the heartless
Buffoon that you are
Drips off your hands
For that

If I don't find you in hell
Then I'll refuse to
Plunge into the flames
I do concede that I am a sinner
But I have not
Enabled COVID-19 to ravage
Two hundred thousand people
Of my land
On my watch

END
©Simon Chilembo, 18/08-2020

BOOK 4

<br>

# EDITED OFF THE CUFF YOUTUBE VIDEO TALKS TEXTS

# CHAPTER 24

✖

# COVID-19: WE SHALL PULL THROUGH
"Know Thyself!"
Edited Youtube Video Talk Text: 23/03-2020[53]

People ask me how is it that I can talk about surviving this Coronavirus crisis period and its challenges.

I say, "We'll pull through. We'll make it. Everything will be alright!"

The people's concern is that I still have not recovered from the knock I got from the Global Financial Crisis of 2008.

That's a valid concern. But I address myself to the choices we make as individuals in hard times. I focus on the thoughts and feelings that motivate us: what we know about ourselves as beings not defined by material trappings of our lives.

The point is that my sense of self-worth is not tied to material objects that I own, or the prestige pertaining thereto. The value of what I own or my perceived status is only in helping me to manoeuvre through the intricacies of life. Therefore, with or without money or lasting wealth the essence of me doesn't change.

If the essence of me does change at all, it can only be that it gets bigger and stronger. That arising from the sense of having become a better person after overcoming specific potentially

---

[53] Simon Chilembo, COVID-19: We Shall Pull Through, https://youtu.be/ MWM861lwi0Q, (accessed July 03, 2020)

destructive challenges in my life. All this being attributable to the work that I do to fortify my mental and emotional states:

- I meditate.

- I pray.

- I research.

- I talk to people.

- I think.

I do lots of things to try to find solutions so that I can keep moving on. It's an endless process. I believe that it'll cease to function only on the day I die. I'm the eternal optimist.

I contend that, indeed, money is everything in our world. Money buys everything. Everything that is of value can sell itself to money. That's how the world works. Until there's a major paradigm shift in the world, lack of money will hinder the fulfilment of basic life needs for many people.

Money may or may not be a passport to happiness in life. But that's as far as it goes for me. With or without money, my intrinsic sense of identity and the values that I stand for do not change. As such, my credibility as a survivor must be judged from the perspective of what my thoughts, my feelings are, and how I articulate them.

Now, as to whether people find me credible or not; or whether they can take me seriously or not, it's up to their understanding, their ways of relating to reality. We have each our references: self-referral objects, belief systems that help us cope with our realities.

It's especially when things fall apart that the essence of you is challenged, both as an individual and as a part of the human collective. That's when your essence calls to you. You don't have to be afraid of things that you can't change to the extent that they don't kill you.

As for me, for as long as I can breathe, I'm alive. And as long as I'm alive, I can create. As long as I can create, I live forever. So, I am convinced that everything will be alright. There's no reason to panic. There's no need to allow oneself to be frightened by all the conspiracy theories that come up in times of crisis. Be strong. Believe in yourself.

If you die, you die. But mankind does have ways of finding solutions to the crises that we come across from time to time. That's part of living. Regarding Coronavirus disease (COVID-19), listen to reason. It's simple; do what serious experts tell you: wash your hands, observe social distancing, wear a mask, amongst others. Much as with conspiracy theories, pay less attention to big politics of the world in which the superpowers – e.g. China, Russia, USA – are in constant rivalries on all fronts.

In the end, you have only yourself to help yourself as an individual. And, then, when you've helped yourself, you can relate to the wider human collective. So, it's on that basis that we've got to regain our strengths as individuals, and as collectives up to the planetary level.

Once we've regained that, then we can move forward; then we can grow, then we can create new things, then we can have the paradigm shifts that elevate us. But until then, NO PANIC! Just relax and have fun. And you can only do what you do.

There'll only be one Albert Einstein. There'll only be one Nelson Mandela. So, you as an individual have got to identify what your essence is all about, how you can help yourself, and from helping yourself you can help others.

Some people, by disposition, by location, by privilege, and many other factors achieve certain things or fail to do certain things. You can only do what you can do to the extent that you are the unique person that you are.

Changing the world, or the ability to adapt to a changing world are functions of how we organize our thoughts and feelings. The golden rule is "Know thyself!"

You've got to find a base, a space that gives you solace, a space that helps you to go into yourself. As long as you live, as long as you breathe, you will find solutions. Have no fear!

Your roots. Look back. How would your ancestors have tackled a situation like this, with their faith or belief systems and modes of living?

# CHAPTER 25

# COVID-19 PERSONAL COPING STRATEGIES

Experience Description Language Use
Edited Youtube Video Talk Text: 13/04-2020[54]

I'd like to talk about personal strategies for coping with challenges accompanying Coronavirus disease outcomes. My talk is going to be based on my COOL COACHING: *Chilembo Optimal Outcomes Life Coaching Principles.*

COOL Coaching has its premise the postulation that in any given situation, you can only do so much – depending on given parameters, tools that can be used, and how to apply those tools.

COOL Coaching is a synthesis of my life experiences as follows, amongst others:

- Academic, professional training.

- Leadership.

- Neuro-Linguistic Programming (NLP).

- Teaching.

---

[54] Simon Chilembo, LANGUAGE AND DESCRIPTION OF EXPERIENCE: COVID-19 OUTCOMES CASE, https://youtu.be/opA2lCiQikw, (accessed July 03, 2020)

NLP looks at how our language use to explain, and also interact with our reality affects our central nervous system and, therefore, conditions our behaviour. Conversely, behaviour also influences how our language develops.

The way we understand and put into words the impact that the current scourge of Coronavirus disease (COVID-19) has on us is important as to whether we'll let it destroy us.

Pertinent questions are:

- Shall we come out of this crisis strong and energized, and ready for take-off when it's over?

- Or are we going to come out down, feeling defeated, and manifesting Post Traumatic Stress Disorder (PTSD) symptoms?

The reality is that this crisis is hard. But how hard is hard?

- Is it so hard that you want to cry and give up?

- Are there new opportunities that the difficult situation can present?

- Perhaps it's merely a necessary pause to give us time to realign our lives?

- Or is it that we are doomed, we are headed for the annihilation of the human race?

It's the words that we choose that will help us come out victorious out of this.

In times like this, we, indeed, use words expressions that reflect our fears, because we don't know, we don't understand what's going on. We feel small.

Change is gonna come. What kind of change? Are we going to be part of this change? Are we going to gain with this change? Or is this change going to destroy us? Those are genuine concerns.

We've lost jobs, we've lost monies – our investment funds through our banks, for example. Is it the end of the world? Those are genuine worry reasons.

Our words hold power. We need to use our language to hold us up. Much like a ship at sea which will encounter rough oceans, it will keep rocking until there is calm. We need to find the words that help us to create and sustain forward-movement, to find the light at the end of the darkness.

Say that it's over now, we are on the other side of Coronavirus disease (COVID-19). What happens, then?

The reality is that there's going to be a new world in more ways than one.

The same elements of uncertainty and insecurity are going to prevail. We are going to be so bruised on the other side; having endured job and wealth losses. Personal relations may also have suffered, with break-ups of families in some cases.

But according to the idea that we are working with here, it all lies in how we explain linguistically, "What is this new situation about?"

You have to address issues of "Who am I? What has become of me?"

Some people will come out of this unscathed. Their jobs, their businesses maybe will be for the better. Even that will cause a major shift in the internal paradigm of the person: their identity – "Who am I?"

Perhaps one of the most important factors touches this very powerful subjective aspect of being human: faith. After so much battering you have to start from scratch.

You've lost face; you are no longer the Super Star that you were in the era before the Coronavirus crisis. You need to question your faith: your beliefs, your God, your ancestral spirits; or whatever it is that nourishes the spiritual aspect of being you.

It's said all the time, "Keep the faith! It's going to be alright!"

If you believe, and you commit yourself to that, you know that it's only a matter of time.

In conclusion, I want to say that opportunities that may arise in the new environment will manifest themselves according to the impressions the mind creates as from the language it processes.

Ahmet Altan, a Turkish writer imprisoned in 2016/17, wrote from isolation in his prison cell, "Like all writers, I have magic. I can pass through walls with ease."[55]

And this is what it's all about. It's magic! Magic making the seemingly impossible possible with your mind, your heart – how you organize your thoughts, how you structure your feelings. That way, telling uplifting stories about this new state of being.

Another line of words of inspiration in this regard reads, "You can travel anywhere, just by closing your eyes."[56]

That shows the importance of allowing oneself to dream. In interpreting your dreams, put words that drive optimism; that feed the faith that "It's going to be alright. We'll rise again. We'll walk through walls. We shall overcome!"

I wish everyone good living, good health, strength; resilience. I haven't forgotten the health professionals and the workers, who are doing such great work in the management of this crisis here. The effort that they make cannot be overemphasized. I am very grateful. I don't forget the volunteers also at all levels. And those who have lost their beloved ones during this crisis, I extend my heart and sympathies.

---

[55] Ahmet Altan, The Writer's Paradox, https://bit.ly/3b8bprX, (accessed 23 June 2020)
[56] Amaryllis Fox, Life Under Cover, https://bit.ly/3fRP0A9, (accessed 23 June 2020)

# ACKNOWLEDGEMENTS

In Norway, my profound appreciation to Saul Sowe, Toril Lefoka, and Regina Molobi for their unwavering love, support, faith, and loyalty. I live in a new, fascinating social relations dynamic in my second phase of life in the country since I returned from South Africa in October 2018.

In this current phase, I'm blessed that some old and new friends live above mediocrity and are ever there in each their respective ways to help me sustain the belief in the good of humanity, despite everything else, ultimately. In this category are included Mimmo Domenico Graziano, Charlie Chirah Abboh, Terje Danielsen, as well as Buntu Pupa.

Others are Trond Furu, Sture Troli, Herolind Shala, Caroline Schønning-Andreassen, Andreas Schønning Andreassen, Chiletso Maggie Skeime, Andrew De Bruin, Henriette Simensen Breilid, Fernanda Serpa Westgaard, Kamaljit Singh Sekhon, Øyvind Bernatek, Baljit Padda Singh, and Bernat Pados, to name but a few. I remain eternally grateful for the faith, love, care, and support.

From Nessoden I draw especially Eyvind Elgesem, Johan Brandt, and Harald Herland for their big hearts, understanding, the spirit of tolerance, and loyalty as friends and former senior Karate students of mine.

Through the above, and together with former *Karate Kids Super Stars* originals like Mattias Jahr, Toril Kværner-Ludvigsen, Lena Grimsrud Aarrestad, Øyvind Dammyr, Fredrik Skurdal, Stein Åke Bjørk, Sigurd Myhra Wiik, and Roger Aanderud-Larsen, I'm convinced that our near quarter-century Karate training play and work were never a wasted effort.

David Bernatek, Elle Cerullo, and Teodor Thyvold stand out from the Oslo *Karate Kids Super Stars* group. As does Hanne Rekkedal, Queen Mother of the group.

To all above, I bow in profound appreciation with the greatest humility and love. Thank you all for some of the best memories of my life. There is ever so much of you in my Norway-state-of-mind existence.

A big thank you to new colleagues and friends in the Forfatterforbundet/*Norwegian Society of Authors* and Oslo Writers League for the warmth, support, and inspiration.

I continue to receive much emotional and spiritual support from Africa and the African Diaspora. Reach outs from especially Doctors Denise Glover and Nawa Sumbwanyambe, as well as musician Ken Simuyemba in the UK are like a prayer. Also in the UK, Oscar Mwanga, PhD, is another source of joy, pride, and intellectual inspiration.

In South Africa, my beloved younger sister *Sisi* Jane Matshidiso Chilembo, keeps the fire burning, playing well her role as the new family matriarch in challenging times for all. I am ever so humble and grateful. As long as my friend-brothers Anele Malumo, Ajit Sam Mangali, Fuad Essack, and H.E. Ambassador Bobby Moroe and their families keep it together, I know that everything is gonna be alright eventually. We just keep breathing and live and let live.

My paternal cousin, Tamara Goma, in Lusaka keeps the link with the land of my father alive. Thank you very much, Ms. Goma! You are loved more than you'll ever know.

Karina Messina Svendsen and Ariel Leficura brought me under their wings in *Oficial* Inthemixstyle media house. They gave me a thought expression platform upon which to develop a now ceased current affairs and social commentaries programme, *Diaspora Magic Talks Show* concept. This has taken my critical thinking and literary creative curiosity and expression to the next level. My gratitude to the couple is immeasurable.

Michael Williams, Victor Mutelekesha, Koubang Mben, and Buntu Pupa guested my programme. They showed but just a tip of the iceberg of the diversity of creative talent and positive force Diasporants bring along with them in their new homelands. Thank you for your support, guys! You are loved.

Despite his hectic schedule amidst dealing with challenges arising from the COVID-19 pandemic socio-economic consequences at work, my Karate teacher and life mentor, *Il Grande Maestro* Professor Stephen Chan, OBE, PhD, kindly took time to look at the original manuscript of this work. As with my previous books, his feedback has elevated the presentational quality of this work. My passion to keep writing towards a thousand books in my lifetime can't help but keep aglow each new day, therefore.

Michelle Bovey-Wood provided an inspiring no-holds-barred Manuscript Evaluation feedback that was a joy to work with. The result is an even more pleasing book to read. My gratitude is unreserved.

I'd also like to thank Adele Wilson of Quickfox Publishing, Cape Town, South Africa. I approached them following the publication gag I received from Amazon in July, 2020. The subsequent professional manner in which she has dealt with this project has impressed me much. So, I sure will *Keep on Penning* – see defiant poem, FALSIFIED, pp. 105–106.

On the occasion of my 60th birthday on June 08, 2020, I received messages of goodwill and well wishes from the cross-section of my family and other personal relations all over the world. My joy and expression of gratitude are beyond words.

Blessed with this much love, I have reason to want to be resolute about continuing to live as a have-no-fear free spirit into the next sixty years of my life and its one thousand books. In the meantime, please join the #simon60000books campaign on social media platforms!

# ABOUT THE AUTHOR

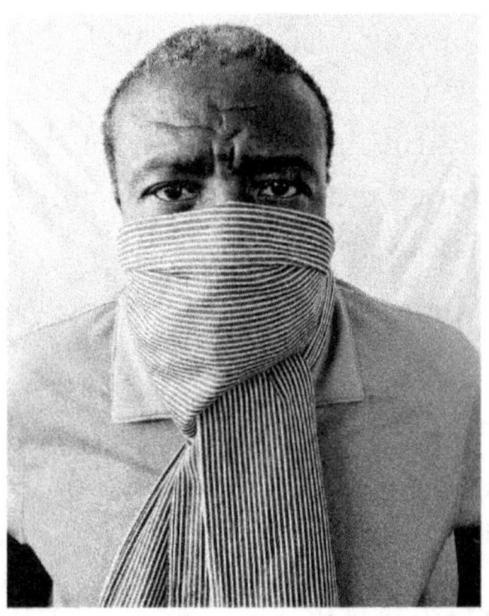

I am a naturalized Norwegian citizen, born in South Africa in 1960. The larger part of my formative years was spent in Lesotho, where I began my schooling career. I lived as an exile in Zambia, my fatherland, between 1975 and 1988. In Zambia, I grew up into a memorable, colourful academic and sports achiever young adulthood. In 1988, I came to Norway to pursue post-graduate studies in economics. This is where I became a man. Love found me here. I stayed. Love shriveled. I live happily ever after.

In a major career change move in the country, I built a reputation for myself as a leading international Karate practitioner and teacher. The two clubs I formed and led in Oslo and Nesodden, respectively, are still operational and are run successfully by my former senior Black Belt students and their protégés. This here is the work of my life the pride of which I'll treasure for as long as I live.

I would subsequently attain professional qualifications in Therapeutic Massage Therapy, Reflexology, and NLP (Neuro-

Linguistic Programming) Master Practitioner Life/Executive Coaching. For more than fifteen years, until June 2013, in connection with the mentioned competencies, I ran a flourishing Health & Wellness practice in Oslo, Norway.

Thank you for buying COVID-19 AND I – *Killing Conspiracy Theories*. The book is the seventh of my many more books to come. This is a continuing fulfilment of dreams to write and publish my own stories and thoughts since my early teenage years. Earlier published books are:

- When the Mighty Fall – *rise again mindgames* (2015)
- Machona – *emigrant* (2016)
- Machona Awakening – *home in grey matter* (2016)
- Machona Son – *ain't going nowhere* (2017)
- Machona Blogs – *as i see it* (2018)
- Machona Mother – *shebeen queen* (2019)

I hold a Bachelor of Arts (BA), Humanities and Social Sciences [African Development Studies (ADS), Economics] degree from The University of Zambia (UNZA), Lusaka. I am also a holder of a 6th Dan Karate Black Belt Master Degree; and I command international Karate pioneer status in three countries, namely, Norway, Zambia, and Zimbabwe.

My hobbies include reading and writing, fitness training, Martial Arts, Health & Wellness, gardening, and urban farming. I also love many aspects of culture: art, music, and theatre. Observing technical and architectural designs inspires me too; as do fashion and style. As a gastrosexual, I enjoy good food and wine in appropriate settings.

I am happily unmarried with no children. However, I have several godchildren that I dearly love.

Blog: www.chilembo.com
Twitter: @simonchilembo

# APPENDIX

⁂

The arguments and structure of their presentation in this book are original. They are a synthesis of my instinctual knowledge; informed and polished by my formal academic education, professional training, as well as my life experience. The validity or falsity of this work in the mind of the reader is my responsibility alone.

My intention and hope are to inspire unfearful objectivity, curiosity, and broad-minded inquiry inclinations. That in times of proliferations of all kinds of information from all kinds of sources in the face of potentially life-threatening natural or man-made catastrophes on our planet and the universe at large.

National, institutional, and private libraries storing huge databases of all aspects of human knowledge in all formats are easily accessible throughout much of the world. People must read!

In our time, the internet has brought the library into the palms of our hands. As a starting point out of a myriad of possibilities, I show below Google and other links with references to resources relevant to the topic covered in this book:

1. COVID-19 resources – https://bit.ly/31JE0kx

2. COVID-19 conspiracy theories:
    (i) Google – https://bit.ly/2NV24ZF
    (ii) AVAAZ – https://bit.ly/3jaXqUQ

3. COVID-19 statistics:
    (i) Worldometer (real time) –
       https://www.worldometers.info/

(ii) nCoV2019.live (real time) – https://ncov2019.live/data
(iii) WHO (World Health Organization) –
https://bit.ly/3fG5Fad

4.  Vaccines:
(i)  CDC – https://bit.ly/3aVJN91
(ii) WHO – https://bit.ly/2EzTHRT

The book is in part edited with Grammarly –
https://grammarly.com/

Also by Simon Chilembo, available on www.amazon.com and other retail outlets: